G000078966

AN ISLAND SHORE

AN ISLAND SHORE
Selected Writings of Robert Rendall

Edited by Neil Dickson

*With a foreword by
George Mackay Brown*

Illustrated by Isobel Gardner

**THE
ORKNEY
PRESS**

Published by The Orkney Press Ltd.,
12 Craigiefield Park, St Ola,
Kirkwall, Orkney.

Published 1990
ISBN 0 907618 25 1
All rights reserved.

Printed in Orkney
by The Orcadian Limited,
Victoria Street,
Kirkwall, Orkney.

Book design by Iain Ashman.

Front cover painting of Robert Rendall
by Ian MacInnes,
photographed by Keith Allardyce.

Back cover painting of Birsay
by Stanley Cursiter,
photographed by Robert P. Rendall, Aberdeen

The publication of this book has
been assisted by financial support
from the Scottish Arts Council and
Orkney Islands Council. The help
of both bodies is warmly
acknowledged, along with the
interest taken and encouragement
given by Mr Walter Cairns,
Literature Director Scottish Arts
Council, and Mr Edwin Eunson,
Convener Orkney Islands Council
1982-90.

FOREWORD

Robert Rendall is one of the outstanding Orkneymen of the twentieth century.

He had a questing mind that took him across far horizons, and always he returned with full and varied cargoes.

I lack knowledge to make any comment on his theological writings, but I was deeply interested in a chapter included in this book that treats of grace and the fruits of Christian living. There is a generosity of spirit there that few good people, of whatever persuasion, could find fault with.

Nor could I say anything of any value about Robert Rendall's contribution to the science of conchology. No doubt it was considerable. The life of the shore was a fascination to him all through his life. Perhaps his happiest days were spent along the Birsay shore, from boyhood onwards.

Archaeology too—"the dark backward and abysm of time"—intrigued him. There is his extraordinary and fortuitous discovery, while painting a picture, of the world-famous Broch of Gurness.

For he was an artist too, and though in art he did not achieve the heights he was to attain in literature, some of his line drawings show a true talent.

A many-faceted mind like Robert Rendall's is a rare thing in this age of ever-narrowing specialisation. Perhaps T.E. Lawrence of Arabia among the moderns possessed it. In

Elizabethan times a few great minds could span all that had been achieved and celebrated in the sciences and arts.

Robert Rendall was a kind of 20th-century Elizabethan. Had his enquiries stopped at the limits I have indicated, that would have been more than enough for most men. But, rather late in life, he "took up" literature; and against all the odds, especially in a mind with a scientific bent, he began to produce poetry of very high quality.

I think it must have been the poets of the Greek Anthology that summoned him (as Keats was summoned a century and a half earlier by a translation of Homer) into "the realms of gold". Whenever in his output of verse the Greeks were his touchstone, he never failed, from his early poem 'The Fisherman' on. *Orkney Variants,* his second book, is crammed with such treasures: pure and perfect transpositions into the Orkney dialect.

He was also, as is perhaps to be expected, influenced by some of the English Georgian poets he read in his youth, and the fruitage of that vineyard is of lesser quality by far.

So we have the curious case of a poet—he resembled Wordsworth in this respect, and perhaps MacDiarmid—whose output was either of the highest quality, or negligible. There seems to be no middle ground in the poetry of Robert Rendall.

He wrote good prose too, as his Diary of an Italian trip shows. A rare delight is his essay on the harvest of bere, with its marvellous touches of humour. He later transmuted this same experience into verse.

Robert Rendall says in that same essay that it was his reading of Virgil and Horace that prompted him to become a crofter near Scapa. The earth as well as the sea was in his blood. Perhaps it is this close intermingling of land and sea that makes a curious kinship between classical Greece and modern Orkney; the Greek element is to be found here and there in Edwin Muir's verse too.

*   *   *

Apart from his scientific and literary gifts, Robert was a delightful companion to be with. He seemed to be overflowing perpetually with a kind of boyish enthusiasm, in which his friends were caught up and carried along. And all he said was leavened with laughter, an upsurge of innocent and wholesome delight . . . It shouldn't be forgotten that for much of his later life he was almost totally deaf, a condition that might have driven most men in upon themselves. Not Robert—he conversed freely and freshly, and seemed to divine what his friends said and meant.

I am very glad that this book is now published. Robert Rendall's verse has long been out of print. It is time, surely, for this great Orcadian to be recognised and honoured. His like will never be again.

GEORGE MACKAY BROWN
Stromness, 19 December, 1989

To Beth

CONTENTS

SELECTED POETRY

from Country Sonnets

from Orkney Variants

from Shore Poems

from The Hidden Land

Uncollected Poems

A SELECT BIBLIOGRAPHY

ILLUSTRATIONS

by Isobel Gardner

by Robert Rendall

EDITOR'S NOTE AND ACKNOWLEDGEMENTS

'Beyond all this,' Robert Rendall wrote of Italy, 'I see an island shore.' Even there, he confessed, 'I was haunted by the tumbling seas of Orkney.' The shore—the meeting of land and sea which is so characteristic of Orkney—occupied his life; those 'other shores' became his metaphor for the presence of the Divine. It is a fitting metaphor for his life and work.

In editing the letters I have corrected the handful of obvious slips of the pen that he made, but the punctuation is substantially his. The exception to Rendall's orthographic consistency is his treatment of Orcadian surnames, place-names and words, and his variations have not been standardised. The text of a number of the letters has been abridged to allow the inclusion of a representative sample of his interests as they emerged in his correspondence. In two cases the draft copies only of the letters have been available to me: the letter to Professor William Barclay and the letters to Sir James Fergusson. Approximate dates have been assigned to these letters on the basis of internal evidence. The same has been necessary with the undated early letters to Ernest Marwick.

The selected prose shows the range of Rendall's interests. It is arranged in chronological order of writing. 'The Literary Uses of Dialect' exists in note form only. I have selected extracts and rearranged the paragraphs. Rendall's words, however, have not been changed.

The belief that Robert Rendall wrote his truest poetry in the Orkney dialect has governed the choice of the poems. Only his two longer dialect poems in *Orkney Variants* ('Mansie's Threshing' and 'Lament for the Legends') have been not been included. Inevitably, some readers will find a favourite poem in English omitted. I can only hope that the inclusions will compensate for the omissions.

Grateful acknowledgement for permission to include copyright material and for providing material in their possession is made to: Mr Robert P. Rendall, Aberdeen, for allowing me to consult freely and quote from the family papers and his uncle's books and papers in his possession, and for permission to include Robert Rendall's published poetry, selections from *Extracts from a Travel Diary,* chapters from *The Greatness and Glory of Christ* and *Orkney Shore,* and to reproduce several of Robert Rendall's drawings in his possession; to Mr John Oddie, sole surviving executor of Robert Rendall's estate; to the Orkney Archive for permission to quote from Robert Rendall's papers (D27), to include his letters to Professor William Barclay, Stanley Cursiter (dated 1949-57), and Sir James Fergusson, and to include extracts from the 'Notes on the Literary Uses of Dialect', and 'The Impartial Sun'; also to the Orkney archive for permission to consult and quote from Ernest Marwick's papers (D31/34/1), and to include letters to him; to George Mackay Brown and the Trustees of the National Library of Scotland for permission to include the letters to George Mackay Brown; to Mrs Margaret Hunter and the Trustees of the National Library of Scotland for permission to include letters to Stanley Cursiter (dated 1959-65); to Mr John Rendall of Holland in Papa Westray for permission to include letters to William Traill of Holland; to the University Library of St Andrews for permission to include the letter to Willa Muir; to Mr John R. Watson and the Christian Brethren Archive, John Rylands University Library of Manchester, for permission to include letters to Mr John R. Watson; to Dr George Mackay Brown for permission to include 'Sonnet: to Robert Rendall' on pp. 38-9; and to Greenwood Press for permission to quote on p.35 the poem by Mr Dudley Fitts.

For the Orkney background I have relied in places upon the writings of three individuals. Patrick Bailey's *Orkney* (David and Charles, 1971 & 1985) and William P. L. Thomson's *History of Orkney* (The Mercat Press, 1987) have provided information on history, society and culture. George Mackay Brown's essays on Orkney, *An Orkney Tapestry* (Gollancz, 1969), *Portrait of Orkney* (The Hogarth Press, 1981), and 'Orkney Literature in the Last Century' (*The Orcadian*, 18 November, 1954, p.2), are indispensable for the literary background.

Several individuals supplied me with information or helped close a line of enquiry: Dr David Bertie, Mr John C. Brown, Professor P. H. Butter, Dr Nancy Cunningham, Sir Charles Fergusson, the late Professor Ronald Miller, Mr Robert P. Rendall, Dr James Thompson, and Mr John R. Watson. I am grateful for the assistance of a number of librarians and archivists. Special thanks must go to those who have been particularly helpful: Miss Alison Fraser and the staff of the Orkney Archive; Mr David Tinch and the staff of the Orkney Library; Dr David Brady of the Christian Brethren Archive; Mr Stanley Simpson of the Department of Manuscripts at the National Library of Scotland; and Mrs Louise Yeudall of Kilmarnock Academy Library.

I am fortunate in having had much generous help in writing this book. I am grateful to Ms Isobel Gardner whose illustrations are an integral part of the text. The enthusiasm and assistance of Mr Howie Firth at The Orkney Press has been indispensable. Dr David Bebbington, Dr George Mackay Brown, Dr Douglas Gifford and Mr John Oddie read the manuscript of the life of Robert Rendall, and made a number of invaluable suggestions. Mr John Oddie has also drawn freely upon his store of knowledge of Robert Rendall and Orkney to answer my numerous enquiries. Mrs Daisy Oddie has shown me how open-handed Orcadian hospitality is. Dr George Mackay Brown has been a continual source of advice and encouragement. I am grateful to him for writing the foreword. Mrs Ella Jack has kindly read the proofs. Finally, thanks to my wife who typed parts of the manuscript, and who has constantly listened, encouraged and advised.

NEIL DICKSON
Kilmarnock, 1990

Beyond it all I see an island shore

'Train Journey'

THE FLOSS, WESTRAY c. 1900

The Life and Work of
Robert Rendall
(1898 - 1967)

Young eyes have glimpsed
God's glory in dandelions

'On a London Street'

Robert Rendall was born in Glasgow on 24 January, 1898. Both his parents came from Westray in Orkney, and the Rendalls can trace their Orcadian ancestry as far back as records will allow. His father, Robert Peterson Rendall, came from at least six generations of weavers. His mother, Barbara Craigie Garrioch, was the daughter of a fisherman who on occasion also did some farm service. There was one ancestor, John Rendall, who had been a schoolmaster in the Wasbister district of Rousay. One summer when making enquiries on Rousay about him, Rendall was told to his amusement by an old woman, 'He was schule-mester, but lazy, lazy. He would leave the bairns tae his wife for their lessons and spend aa his time at the loom.' It was this John Rendall who, despite his reputation for laziness, later moved with his family to Westray.

Rendall's father, born in 1866, was raised on the Floss, the family croft near the Sand o' Gill. Known in the family as Bob, he was the third child of six, and the croft was unable to support them all. When their father died, and the croft fell to the oldest brother, the younger sons had to leave. It was a time of economic hardship and high emigration in Orkney. One of the brothers, Thomas, had already gone to Chicago in 1888, but he had found little work, and within eight months had died. Opportunities in the islands were restricted for ambitious young men, but Thomas's unfortunate history cast a shadow, for a time at last, over the attractions of overseas emigration. Bob Rendall went to sea, sailing at first on local voyages. In 1890, along with his younger brother William, he left for Leith to obtain a berth on a foreign-going ship. He was hard-working and intelligent, and although his early education had been limited, by studying in his spare time he was able to obtain his master's certificate at the age of thirty-three. He married Barbara Garrioch in 1895, and his wife moved to Glasgow to be near him when his ship was in port. But even so, he was often away on lengthy voyages. Robert's earliest memories of his father were of an intimidating though kindly stranger 'who brought magic curios home to us, bark-canoes from Canada, knob-kerries and shark's jaws from Africa, curious inlaid banks from China or Japan, and scrumptious Turkish delight.'

The Glasgow into which Robert Rendall was born was a city of tenements, factories and industrial bustle. Yet from an early age he was aware of an affinity with nature. His first memory of unrestricted countryside was on a Sunday School picnic, though it was not the excitements of the jaunt that he was to remember but the astonishment of seeing a hawthorn hedge in full bloom. 'That,' he later wrote, 'became the world I instinctively reached after, though from the limited outlook given by a high tenement window (below which was only the court with its drab brick ashpits and wash-houses) my only view of freedom was the inaccessible landscape of the sky.' The Rendalls lived in Old Dumbarton Road, near to the entrance to Kelvingrove Park, and his mother took him and his brother William on daily walks in the park and, on rainy days, into the Art Galleries and Museum. The stuffed animals of the Museum filled him with wonder and they became part of the rich interior world which he inhabited as a child. Capturing the beauty of line and form that he instinctively detected in animals became an obsession in his drawing of fishes and birds in flowing strokes. But it was not only the high tenements of Glasgow that forbade direct contact with nature: park-keepers were always present to enforce prohibitions against touching the flowers.

Robert's health was poor and the pollution of Glasgow only made it worse. Three different doctors advised his mother that the boy would not live a year; and so in 1905, when Robert was just seven, she took him back to her native Orkney. She settled in Kirkwall, living at first in Victoria Street and then in School Place. Anticipating another change that Orkney would bring, his father wrote from Japan, 'You will be able to have a run round there.' Rendall began his autobiographical *Orkney Shore* with a description of this change:

> My earliest memory of Orkney is of a boy of seven standing in a field of daisies at Pipersquoy. The moment is etched in my mind, and I can still recall the uneasy apprehension with which I looked first this way and then that before stooping down to pick the flowers. Though I did not know it at the time it was my first experience of natural freedom.

Although his health as a child was to remain delicate, Rendall felt he owed his physical existence to Orkney; and there were other senses in which he owed his life to the islands. He was later to learn how his experience was the reverse of Edwin Muir's. In 1901 the Muir family had left Orkney for Glasgow. Within five years both Muir's parents and two of his brothers were dead, while he himself lived on oppressed by the city's industrial squalor. The fall from Eden was to become the central preoccupation of Muir's imagination but, wrote Rendall,

> His was an exile from island to city, an expulsion involving a journey back; mine, an early escape into freedom, and in the islands themselves, to its edge by the shore. Glasgow had been to me, boy as I was, a vast terror-filled jungle, which by its very immensity and swarms of people was too much to take in. One had to be alert. But when I came to Orkney, life became more manageable. I found myself moving within a recognisable pattern of living. People were spaced out, and there was a landscape that allowed distance. This was life as it should be.

The sense of Orkney as an entrance into the natural inheritance of humanity, Paradise regained, never left Robert Rendall.

It was the Orkney shore in particular which drew him. His

father's occupation had thrust the family back on Barbara Rendall, and it is a testimony to her care that he remembered his childhood as a time of great happiness. She continued Robert's contact with the natural world that she had begun in Glasgow. On fine summer evenings she would meet her two boys coming from school and would take them for a picnic at a beach. After the picnic, the boys would ramble along the shore, taking their finds home for display in glass-topped cardboard boxes. During the summer holidays they would go to their grandfather's croft on Westray, where Robert found it an enchanting experience to sleep in a traditional Orkney box-bed with tin pails on its wooden top to catch the rain that dripped through the leaky roof of flagstones and divots; or their mother would send them to stay with Janet Couper of the Lower Palace in Birsay. Here the shore was immediate and Robert and his brother explored it continually. Trout and eels were fished for, and crabs, whelks and starfish were gathered. 'The Orkney summers of my boyhood,' he later wrote, 'are a memory of infinite Saturday afternoons spent in the fields or on some foreshore near Kirkwall, an illusion of timelessness lost in later years.'

There was one other way in which Rendall's mother deeply influenced his future development. In a letter to a friend after her death he described his mother as being 'a practical but devout woman, of unselfish character, strict but kind with us in our upbringing'. She had joined the Salvation Army after undergoing an Evangelical conversion while in domestic service in Orkney, but in Glasgow she became a member of the Christian Brethren to which her husband's family belonged. The Brethren in Scotland grew in the wake of the late nineteenth-century Evangelical revivals, and their piety showed this origin. They attempted to return to the unity and order of the early church; they had no official clergy, and church life was maintained entirely by the artisans and lower middle-class individuals who composed the membership of their self-governing congregations. Rendall's earliest memories of all were of their weekly communion services where his mother began to take him while he was still a baby. The solemnity of the Sunday evening evangelistic services of his boyhood was to remain for him 'a permanent experimental assurance of the objective truth of Christianity'. It was while in Glasgow that he heard Henry Pickering, owner of a prominent Christian publishing firm, giving a children's talk that led him to make a faith-commitment to Christ at the age of seven. But his mother's influence lay behind his early decision and he attributed it largely to her prayers and training at home. It was the beginning of a life-long identification with the Evangelical faith in its Brethren form.

The family's move to Kirkwall meant that opportunities to see the father were even more limited. In August 1909 he was writing to Robert in mid-Atlantic during a voyage to China, 'it will soon be two years since I left you on Scapa Pier. When we are to see each other again is more than I can say.' Life at sea was hard, and conditions varied from ship to ship, depending on the vessel or the captain and the crew. Rendall did not want either of his sons to follow him, and, he wrote to Robert, 'my advice to you is, don't go to sea. I don't wish either of you to go to sea, as I know quite well what kind of life it is. You will tell Willie that he had not to dream of going to sea.' In fact it was to be another six months before he was to see his family again. He applied for sick leave at the beginning of 1910 and was able to have a holiday in Orkney with his family. He had written to his wife earlier, 'It is hard to know what is best to do. I am getting about full up of this sort of life, it is neither one thing or another for you or me.'

Bob Rendall was a man given to strong feelings. It was not only the conditions aboard ship and the separation from the family that he found frustrating. Both Robert and William were doing well at school and he wanted to give them a better start in life than his own. To be able to support them he felt that he had to stay at sea. He had had his master's certificate for ten years, but he still did not have his own ship, and the lack of further advancement he found annoying. As he sailed back to the East in the summer of 1910 he felt increasingly melancholic. 'I am sorry sometimes,' he wrote to his wife, 'that we did not take a farm & stayed home when I was at home or tryed some thing else.' His younger brother William had emigrated to New Zealand, and Rendall wondered 'what prospect there would be for the boys out there.' He lamented, 'I should have written to him when I was at home.' And his poor prospects of promotion still occupied his mind. He was finding life very bleak.

Ironically it was on this voyage—his last—that he finally achieved his ambition. On the journey home he had to take command of the ship when the captain, who had spent most of the voyage drunk, was put ashore in Aden after drinking a bottle of perfume. The circumstances in which Rendall had to take command, and the exertion of unloading the cargo, proved too much for him. By the time he reached the house of some friends in Edinburgh he was in a deep depression, and Barbara Rendall was sent for. She had little money for the journey and did not realise how ill her husband was, but nevertheless she went. Before they boarded the train to begin the journey north, Rendall had to be restrained from throwing himself in front of a moving locomotive. He stayed with the family in Kirkwall for a few months, but one day Robert found his father shortly after he had attempted to cut his own throat. Rendall was committed to the Royal Mental Hospital, Aberdeen where he died three years later in 1914 at the age of forty-seven. It was found that he had had a brain tumour. His body was brought home to be buried in Orkney. The expenses were paid for out of poor relief.

SCHOOL PLACE, KIRKWALL c. 1915

Finding his father after the attempted suicide was a terrible shock to Robert's nerves, and it left him with a fear of mental instability. He had never really known his father, and the circumstances of his death meant that he would be seldom talked about. In his letters Rendall had constantly exhorted Robert to do well at school, but there was little chance of that now. The year his father was committed to hospital, Robert left school. He was only thirteen. An uncle of his father's had founded a draper's business in Kirkwall, George Rendall & Co.

(situated at The Brig where Albert Street joins Bridge Street). It was still owned by family relatives, and Robert was given employment in the shop. The family's straitened financial circumstances had made his leaving school necessary, but for many years it was a source of bitterness to him that he had been unable to continue his education. Their poverty and the need to support the family, however, had isolated Robert from the social forces which often took people out of the islands. It was the frustration of both his father's hopes for him and his own early ambitions that kept him in Orkney at a critical stage in his development.

In 1916, mid-way through the First World War, Robert was called up. But even then he did not have to leave Orkney. He joined the Royal Navy and was posted as an officers' steward on HMS *Imperieuse*, which was anchored in Longhope Bay, Hoy. This ship was a supply vessel and post-office for the Grand Fleet which had its main base in Scapa Flow during the war. Although he was in the Navy for three years, his posting meant that he avoided combat. The cheerful enthusiasms and independence that often led him to disregard conventional appearance began to be in evidence. A group of Christians were meeting on the ship to witness to their faith and for mutual strengthening, despite the resulting disapproval and obloquy, and Robert became their preacher. His continued interest in natural history almost got him into trouble once when he forgot about a sea urchin which he had hidden away and which began to smell rather foully. The entire crew was turned out to find the malodorous source and it was only then that Robert remembered the hidden specimen. A cabbage he had in his locker was blamed and he discreetly got rid of the real culprit later.

> *This kingdom, too, is ours, and in our blood*
> *Its passionate tideways run*
>
> 'Orkney'

Despite the difficulties of his earlier years, Robert Rendall was fortunate in that the two major interests of his life were in place by an early age: his faith and Orkney. As a natural and social environment Orkney has a unique character, and his life

23

can only be understood against it and the influence of his faith. He explored them both with immense zest.

After the War he roamed across much of Orkney, traversing its moorlands and hill-tops, but it was always to the shore and its life that he returned. He was fascinated by marine zoology, and he studied it where it was accessible on the shore. Conchology—the study of shells and the molluscs that inhabit them—became his special interest.

Orkney forms a distinctive marine ecology. Its waters derive their special character from the fact that the islands are separated from mainland Scotland by deep water and they rest on a shelf, which means that the inshore waters are, at their deepest, only two hundred feet. In addition, Orkney divides the Atlantic from the North Sea and, as Rendall discovered, its waters combine characteristics of eastern and western coastal seas. He was led to this theory because for most of his life he searched two beaches regularly: the Birsay shore between Marwick Head and the Brough of Birsay, which is open to the Atlantic; and the point of Carness opposite Thieves Holm where the Orkney waters mix with the waters of the North Sea. By searching these beaches after gales and spring ebb tides, he was able to obtain information on shells on both coasts. As well as demanding an ability in scientific classification, the task required dedication and patience. But Rendall approached it with characteristic enthusiasm and inventiveness. To help in gathering specimens from remoter islands he devised a shell-collecting competition for children which gave him what he needed and at the same time provided involvement in natural history, and a reward, for them.

During his teens, to finance his interests Rendall had entered Kirkwall horticultural competitions, sometimes winning all first three prizes. He was also interested in wild flowers, and shortly after he had begun their study, he visited the botanist and schoolmaster, Magnus Spence of Deerness, with some specimens he had found at Papdale for identification. To his delight he was told that he had discovered a sub-species of Lady's Smock until then unknown in Orkney. Spence presented him with a signed copy of his *Flora Orcadensis* (1914), and standing by the schoolmaster's study table Rendall determined in himself that he would one day write a book with a Latin title on Orkney molluscs. He had already, partly with the help of his brother William, built up a collection of shells. It was probably soon after the meeting with Spence that he began their systematic study, for in a letter to Stanley Cursiter he dated its beginning to 15 October, 1916.

Magnus Spence was in the long tradition of Orkney naturalists who had devoted themselves to the study of the natural history of the islands. There had been men such as the Rev. George Low, whose work covered all the natural sciences and included drawings from microscope work of the highest quality; Professor Thomas Traill, editor of the 8th edition of the Encyclopaedia Britannica, who built up an outstanding collection of Orcadian fossil fish; Dr William Balfour Baikie (the explorer of the Niger) and Robert Heddle who jointly wrote the first part of a comprehensive natural history of Orkney; and John G. Iverach, who brought together in a systematic form the growing records of local marine zoology. In the twentieth century the islands produced a number of distinguished scientists at various universities throughout the English-speaking world, and Rendall regarded this as 'the flowering of an earlier island tradition'. His own potential as a naturalist was recognised in Orkney, and one day in Kirkwall in the late twenties, when he was walking past the library in Laing Street, a stranger hailed him from its steps. It was the laird of Papa Westray, William Traill of Holland, himself a keen naturalist. Traill had heard of Rendall's interest in molluscs, and without further introduction he launched into a history of Orcadian naturalists. They became friends and Rendall often visited him in Papa Westray and was taken on excursions round the island on the laird's pony and trap. The existence of the Orkney tradition in natural science and his acceptance into it was important to Rendall: years later he closed his *Orkney Shore* with a history of it.

The association of draper's assistant and laird in a common heritage was possible because of the special character of Orcadian society. In the earlier years of the twentieth century Orkney culture and society was still remarkably homogenous. The divisions among classes that were to be found elsewhere in Britain were largely absent from the islands. Edwin Muir remembered that when the Duke of York (later George V) was in Orkney, a group of boys among whom Muir was standing did not take off their caps because such deference was unknown to them. The islands had developed their own culture, blending Norse and Scottish influences, in isolation from the rest of Britain, and Orcadians were acutely aware of this distinctiveness.

25

There were also a number of literate individuals even in the remoter parishes; the library in Kirkwall (founded in 1683) claims to be the oldest lending library in Britain. Rendall continued his education through its shelves while the Kirkwall bookseller, George Leonard, whose shop was just across the street, gave him much early encouragement.

The tradition of studying the natural history of Orkney was paralleled by an Orcadian tradition of studying the human history of the islands. The translations of the *Orkneyinga Saga* made from the late nineteenth century onwards gave Orcadians a unique window into their own past. Orkney is rich in archaeological sites and during the latter half of the nineteenth century Orcadians like George Petrie the Sheriff Clerk, Dr William Traill and R. S. Clouston had helped discover and excavate them. The Orkney Antiquarian Society, founded in 1922, became the focus for the study of the human history of Orkney in the nineteen-twenties and thirties. J. Storer Clouston who studied Norse history, Hugh Marwick who was then embarking on his study of the Orkney Norn and Orkney place-names, and John Mooney, the historian who made Kirkwall and Orkney religious history his special study, were the leading scholars involved in the founding of the Society. There were several others, such as Duncan J. Robertson who collected Orkney folklore, who were also capable of giving a lead in matters of scholarship.

It was John Mooney who introduced Rendall to the Society when he asked him to draw a ground plan of the Cathedral to illustrate a paper he was working on. It was only later that Rendall realised that this was Mooney's way of drawing him into the Society. With self-deprecating humour he later compared finds in unlikely places with John Mooney's discovery of himself: 'The possibility of finds in "kitchen middens" was one of the things that he was always seeking to impress upon the minds of young people.' Once in the Society Rendall found it congenial. There was something almost boyish in the enthusiasm with which the members listened to and discussed matters of mutual interest. The uncovering of further buildings at Scarabrae (Rendall's spelling) in 1925, for instance, and the fresh excavation of the site by Gordon Childe, added to the sense of the importance of the Society's work. In its history which he later wrote Rendall described the atmosphere of the Society as being that of 'a happy band of brothers', and this meeting of eager minds, which admitted him as an equal, stimulated him immensely.

Younger members of the Society were pressed to join in the work of preserving and exploring Orkney's past. Rendall in his island wanderings helped Hugh Marwick in his study of Orkney place-names, but again it was William Traill of Holland who took Rendall under his wing. He took him to see the recently discovered earth-house at Rennibister and taught him how to make plans of an archaeological site. It was this training that Robert Rendall put to good use when in 1929 the leg of his painting-stool sank into a hole in the ground on a knowe near the point of Gurness in the parish of Evie. He did a rough survey of the mound and fixed on a point for an inspection pit. He described what happened next:

> By sheer good luck the first thrust of the spade uncovered
> what proved to be the top opening of a narrow stone
> stairway set between solid walls. The inner wall, however,
> was of heavy flagstone, and by shining a torch between the
> chinks I could see that there were chambers of some kind
> behind it. A boy from the farm assisted me. As I
> progressed down step by step, he lowered a bucket on a

BROCH of GURNESS–DURING EXCAVATION

rope so that I could fill it with the loose debris for him to draw up. I managed to clear about seven steps but, afraid of impending collapse of the inner wall upon me, I ceased from further excavation.

A few calculations based on what he had learned from Traill established that he had found the site of a broch. The subsequent excavation by professional archaeologists found the remarkably well preserved out-buildings and inner tower of the broch of Gurness, one of the two most impressive broch sites discovered in Orkney.

Further archaeological surveys followed. A field on the Kirkwall-Stromness road near Quanterness had been ploughed for the first time in the autumn of 1929, and, knowing the likelihood of finding implements on newly-ploughed land, Rendall walked across the field and found a leaf-shaped arrowhead. He did a more systematic investigation with James Tulloch, his closest friend during this period, and was able to establish from the numerous chippings and flint cores that the site had been a flint floor or a Stone Age 'factory' for making flint implements. The results of this find at Wideford Hill were presented in a paper to the Orkney Antiquarian Society in 1930. Some time after this, Thomas Linklater of South Ettit in the parish of Rendall approached him with the flints he had collected while farming. Rendall passed on the findings to an expert in London and the report Rendall received from him demonstrated that the flints were the earliest artefacts yet found in Orkney. Again the findings were written up in a paper for the Society.

The interest in Orkney prehistory and in the ways it could be studied through archaeology and folklore reflected movements that were common to contemporary European civilisation. Rendall for one was always aware of this larger perspective. He had gone to night school to learn German, and during the 1930s he visited Germany on a number of occasions. His early experience of Glasgow, he claimed, had given him an awareness of the wider world. And there were other influences at work too. In his library reading he had come across the natural histories of the Victorian amateur naturalists, whose works were filled with Classical allusions and references to European and English literature. Their work represented an ideal which influenced him profoundly. 'The impression left after dipping into such volumes,' he wrote in *Orkney Shore,* 'is that of cultured minds living a whole life and refusing to be cramped within the narrow confines of specialised knowledge.' Closer to home, the example of Hugh Miller, the Cromarty stone-mason who became famous in the nineteenth century for his geological studies and his religious journalism, was consciously imitated by him.

It was his interest in Brethren European missionary work that had taken Rendall to Germany initially, for the Brethren Bible school at Wiedenest was the focus of his visits. On his second visit to Germany in 1932 he travelled with his cousin, John Laughton, but before they set off a mutual uncle attempted to dissuade them from going because of the rising power of Hitler. Undoubtedly Rendall was aware of the threat that Hitler posed, because of his contact among the Brethren in Germany. Independent Evangelical groups such as the Brethren were viewed unfavourably by Hitler and he ordered changes in their church organisation in an attempt to keep their activities under his control. But once they were on their own Rendall asked Laughton, 'What's to hinder us from going?' and so they went.

One evening in Germany they found themselves sharing their hotel dining-room with a Nazi Party gathering. As he watched them march in to the part of the room curtained off for their use, Rendall conceived the notion that he would like to take a Swastika badge home as a souvenir of his trip. The head porter, a keen Nazi, told Rendall where the local headquarters were. Rendall and Laughton arrived in the middle of a Party conference. The request was impossible, they were told, and they were hastily ushered from the building. The bravado of Rendall's actions may now seem politically naive, but it was an attempt to show his feelings about Nazi authoritarianism.

At Wiedenest Rendall met religious refugees from Russia and was impressed by the number of languages some people could speak while being ashamed of British insularity. He used the visits to extend his knowledge of the visual arts. When in France on his first visit to Europe in 1930, he visited the Louvre and Versailles, and on subsequent visits he regularly visited other art galleries and museums. The whole experience that the Antiquarian Society had given him of contact with educated minds, of individual investigation and the systematic presentation of data, had provided Rendall with an invaluable training.

29

His continental travel, like the rest of his informal education, gave his mind a wider culture.

> *Constant beyond all change of sky or soil,*
> *Lies fenced the mystery of the living shoot—*
> *Green involutions of the mind.*

'Renewal'

The visits to Germany were stopped by the Second World War. By now he was inclined to pacifism. He had been brought to this through discussions with John Mooney whose biography of St Magnus had portrayed the Saint as being an early Christian pacifist; and in all probability Rendall's pacifism was reinforced by a strong tradition of it in the Brethren. The question of active service did not arise for him, however, because of his age. He bought a croft, Northbank, in Scapa. There were several reasons for this: whatever his attitude to war itself was, he was a determined anti-Fascist and farming was partly his way of contributing to the nation's weal; and it was also a way of entering into Orkney country life. During the war then, he cultivated the land, and in doing so he recovered the peace and the sense of timelessness of his childhood. It was this experience which issued in the publication late in 1946 of his first book of poems, *Country Sonnets*.

Rendall had always been a keen reader of poetry, particular favourites being *The Greek Anthology*, Matthew Arnold and Robert Bridges. *Country Sonnets* clearly showed the influence of his reading, particularly the poets of the early twentieth century, the Georgians. Along with poems that alluded to Classical literature, the book had others whose subject-matter comprised the familiar themes of Georgian poetry. Rendall had, in fact, written poetry from his teens. Most of his early work he had destroyed, but the earliest poem in the book, 'David the Shepherd', was written in 1917 or 1918, and about half of the others were written during the twenties and thirties though with frequent later revisions.

The poems received a warm reception in Orkney. Dr Hugh Marwick had contributed a foreword to the book and the first impression of five hundred copies was sold within a fortnight. They were enthusiastically received by *The Orkney Herald's* reviewer, George Mackay Brown, in a review entitled 'Orcadian Classical Poetry'. 'As far as I can remember,' he wrote, 'this is the first time that Orkney life has been described by a classical cultured mind deriving from Virgil and Theocritus.' The response was sufficiently encouraging to try a wider audience, and Stanley Cursiter, the Kirkwall-born painter, encouraged Rendall to send a copy of the book early in 1947 to his friend James Fergusson (later Sir James) at *The Glasgow Herald.*

Fergusson welcomed *Country Sonnets.* It suited his tastes in poetry exactly, and he reviewed it in glowing terms in 'Arts Review' on the Scottish Home Service and then, more cautiously, a few days later in *The Glasgow Herald.* 'His book contains more promise,' he said on the radio, 'than any first book of poems I have seen published since Hugh MacDiarmid's *Sangschaw*—with which, I should add, it has very little else in common.' The mention of MacDiarmid was significant, for during a radio debate the previous year Fergusson had dubbed the language used by MacDiarmid and his poetic followers 'plastic Scots'. *Country Sonnets,* however, supported his own feelings about poetry. He gave Rendall valuable advice on where to send it for review and it was noticed favourably in a number of different places. Criticisms were made though, for Georgian poetry was then a vanishing fashion, and in addition it was felt by some reviewers that the verse was at times derivative.

The criticisms were not without substance. Georgian poetry was a poetry of escape from the city to the country, one of the reasons for its appeal for Rendall. On the dust-jacket of *Country Sonnets* he claimed: 'These poems interpret against an Orcadian background the perennial urge in man's heart towards a life in the country . . . They express the revolt of the human spirit against the repressions of our modern mechanistic civilisation.' At its worst, however, Georgian poetry chose themes which were thought to be somehow especially poetical; the danger was that the poetry often became an exercise, bland and lacking convicition. *Country Sonnets* demonstrated these faults at times. Many of the poems merely echoed Robert Bridges, Walter de la Mare and Edmund Blunden. All these difficulties can be seen in, for instance, the final stanza of 'The Praise of Beauty':

> I will not heed your whisperings
>   That Beauty's rapture may be crossed;
> That, where she wanders, no one sings,
> And that the loveliness of things
>   Dies loverless and lost.

But the poems were well crafted: Rendall could handle metre and a simple diction, and he had learned economy of construction from the Classical lyric. And there was one lyric, 'The Fisherman', written in Orkney dialect, that stood out from the rest. George Mackay Brown hailed it in his review as 'the best Orkney dialect poem in existence'. Based on an Andrew Lang translation of Leonidas of Tarentum, a Greek poet of the third century BC, it was this poem which pointed the way forward to Rendall's future development.

It was Robert Rendall's ability to express himself simply in technically accomplished verse that had made James Fergusson welcome his poetry so warmly. Fergusson's tastes in poetry, like Rendall's, were conservative, and this no doubt was a factor in the appeal *Country Sonnets* had for him. But he also recognised that 'The Fisherman' had an excellence of its own. He called it in his review in *The Glasgow Herald* 'such a masterpiece of its kind that one would like Mr Rendall to pursue this vein further.' He echoed this comment in the encouragement he gave Rendall in the correspondence that had sprung up between them. 'I have a feeling,' he wrote to Rendall about the dialect poetry, 'that you might achieve your greatest individuality in that medium, even if only you have so few competitors.' Rendall had followed keenly the controversy over 'plastic Scots' as it raged in 1946 in letters to *The Glasgow Herald*. Orkney speech was rich in words and locutions which blended Norse and Scots influences, and the controversy had kindled his interest in using it as a poetic language. At first it seems that he started almost in jest, but he soon found that it had a liberating effect on his writing. These new dialect poems appeared in 1951 in *Orkney Variants*. On its publication Sir James Fergusson wrote to him: 'One feels the conviction that here is a new voice, singing in perfect confidence and freedom, with "salt i' the bluid".'

His dialect poetry demonstrated his ambivalent response to history. He welcomed science and its methods. As a naturalist he accepted the fossil evidence (sometimes a problem for Christians of a previous generation), and he was keen to follow the new directions ecological studies were taking. 'Historical development cannot be ignored,' he wrote in the context of the displacement of British minority languages by English. But his dialect poetry was an attempt to preserve a past whose disappearance he regretted. Interest in dialect, he believed, was a mark of reverence (his word for this was 'piety') for local culture, and dialect poetry was particularly suited to capturing vanishing ways of thought. In some notes he made at the time he wrote:

> Local piety lingers round declining native tradition, and seeks to preserve in memory the last accents and vital glances of ancestral heritage. Sentiment therefore not infrequently ousts sober judgment, and only when a firm grip is kept on sensibility do poetical expressions of feeling have literary distinction. Poems in the vernacular live when they are actual transcripts of contemporary life; when, though they may characterise a fast-disappearing communal life, they are shot through with the timeless and elemental in human experience . . .

Such ways of thinking about the relationship between dialect and community could, of course, run the risks of 'Kailyard' rural sentimentalisation, of the kind all too prevalent in turn-of-the-century fiction and poetry. Rendall was well aware of the dangers. What he was searching for was an expression of the disappearing present that would also be timeless, of the particular that would be universal. It can be seen in his poem about a kailyard, 'The Planticru'. The poem depicts an old woman tending a planticru, a low-walled Orkney kailyard, occasionally stopping to look out to sea. The final couplet quietly universalises the situation:

> Nor kens hoo firm she haads b'siklike toil
> Man's aald inheritance o' sea and soil.

The myopic, trivialising outlook of the Kailyard tendency is transcended by the vision of humanity's riches.

'The Planticru', however, is not among the very best of the lyrics—it strikes the occasional wrong note—but the first of the new dialect poems written in 1947, 'Cragsman's Widow', was considered by Sir James Fergusson in his letter to Rendall on the publication of the poems to be 'almost if not quite the best thing you have ever done'. Inspired by memories of hearing about the exploits of cragsmen in Westray when he was a boy, it enshrines a vanished way of life while capturing humanity's stoical endurance in the face of nature's indifference. Fergusson's qualifications are justified, for Rendall wrote several poems during the late 1940s that can be placed alongside 'Cragsman's

Widow'. His use of dialect was an essential part of these descriptions of Orkney life. Dialect, Rendall believed, was a 'manuscript of local history', and he established a range of words and idioms still in use, in order to give expression in his poetry to the human consciousness that history had shaped. He was probably influenced in this belief by the work of Hugh Marwick who was using Orkney place-names as a guide to the successive stages of human settlement in the islands.

The place where Rendall felt closest to the ancient Orkney ways was in Birsay in the north-west mainland. 'Birsay,' he wrote in a letter to James Fergusson, 'is *the* place in Orkney where there is a genuine sense of escape from the sophistications of modern life.' It was here that he had spent some of the happiest moments of his childhood, staying with Janet Couper who kept a tea-room and was renowned for her kindly hospitality. It was in Birsay too, according to George Mackay Brown, that he first began to read the Greek poets and the Norse sagas. He had made friends with James Linklater, a beachcomber and keen fisherman, and Willie Harvey, a crofter with a great love of the sea. Rendall accompanied both men on their fishing trips and he later wrote poems about each man. It is figures such as these who stand behind 'Aald Jeems o' Quoys', the fictional subject of the first dialect poem. Among the gentle and courteous crofter-fishermen of this community, free from the competitiveness of much of industrial society, he felt at home and obtained his deepest inspiration.

Because he felt dialect was suitable for portraying fast-disappearing local ways of life, Rendall considered that the soliloquy, in which the speaker gives voice to his or her thoughts, was an appropriate form, and three of his most successful lyrics of this period are of this sort: 'Cragsman's Widow', 'By wi' the Sea' and 'Salt i' the Bluid'. This last poem also contains elements of the fantastic. Rendall considered what William Soutar called 'whigmaleeries'—whimsically fantastic conceits—to be endemic to the Scottish mind. The space poems in MacDiarmid's early lyrics were related to this type of poetry, and Rendall admired poems such as 'The Bonnie Broukit Bairn'. In the imaginatively powerful 'Celestial Kinsmen' (and in one of the English poems, 'The Horse-Mill') Rendall, too, used astronomical imagery. MacDiarmid's universe was that of Pascal's eternal silence of infinite spaces. But Rendall, following earlier models, had in these poems a pre-Copernican world where the mythology expressed the kinship of the heavens with man.

There was one other use he believed dialect was particularly suitable for, and that was translation. There is a long tradition in Scots of verse translation which Rendall was aware of, and he appreciated the efforts of contemporary practitioners of the art such as Douglas Young. It was Douglas Young who, in the notes to his anthology *Scottish Verse, 1851-1951* (1951), described Rendall as 'an enthusiast for the making and translation, collection and criticism of verse in various tongues'. Rendall's preferred name for the type of translation where the details are transposed from one language and culture into another—so that a wine jar becomes a pail of milk—was a 'variant'. Half of the dialect poems were of this sort and it was these 'Orkney variants' which gave the second poetry book its title.

Most of them were translations of lyrics in *The Greek Anthology*. This anthology was based on a collection of early Greek poems made by Meleager of Gadara in the first century BC. His collection was subsequently added to until it came to include some six thousand shorter Greek poems dating from the seventh century BC until the tenth century AD. In 1927 Rendall had compiled his own selection of translations from *The Greek Anthology* by various poets, copying them into a small notebook in his meticulous handwriting. Among this early selection were several that Rendall later turned into Orkney variants. Many of the translations in the notebook were self-consciously literary (seen, for instance, in Lang's translation of 'The Fisherman': Not with the well-manned galley laboured he;/ Him not the Star of the Storms, nor sudden sweep/ Of wind with all his years hath smitten and bent.'), and in his later variants Rendall used a more literal translation. He described their genesis in a letter to James Fergusson: 'They were suggested by strict translation in English but are not intended—as you will readily see—to be literal equivalents in our Orkney dialect, but rather a translation of ideas than of words.'

Rendall's point can be seen by considering Dudley Fitts' paraphrase of an epigram by Lucilius:

On Envious Diophôn

> Diophôn was crucified:
> But, seeing beside him another loftier cross,
> He died of envy.

In Rendall's variant, Lucilius's epigram becomes:

Envy

> Young Magnus wi' the muckle teeth
> For very madrum's deid:
> His brither sheep-thief dirls beneath
> A higher gallows-heid.

The epigram's details have been transferred into historical Orcadian terms, and in doing so Rendall has created a vigorously fresh poem, while successfully capturing the satirical humour of Lucilius.

In his dialect poetry Rendall was exploring the themes of Scottish literature—the community voice, the haunted landscape, the fantastic, Edenic harmony—and the uses of Scots vernacular such as translation and the lyric. It is partly this which gives such a small body of poems their large compass. Nonetheless, Rendall used the Scottish tradition—as he used Greek and English influences—to express the significance of Orkney. One of the reasons Greek poetry appealed to him was that in it he met the same pastoral society which he felt still existed in Orkney: the presentation of pastoral life in the Greek poets had been a factor in his decision to take up crofting.

In the islands his poetry was popular and he achieved the status of an unofficial poet laureate. This was a role he relished. Robert Kemp, the dramatist, recalled the experience of walking through Kirkwall with him while he loudly recited his latest poem in his high clear voice. Unfortunately, it did not always inspire him to his best poetry, and even in *Orkney Variants* there are 'public' poems such as 'The Orkney Primula' which hardly rise above the level of doggerel. In the islands, Rendall felt, there was not the same division between artist and audience that there was elsewhere. 'Writers who address an unknown public,' he once said in a radio interview in 1960, 'cannot have the same satisfaction that we have here in Orkney of writing for our own folk whom we know and meet with day by day.' He aspired to speak for the ordinary Orcadian. Great poetry, he believed, should be capable of being appreciated by both academic and worker, and one of his chief complaints against contemporary poetry was its obscurity. 'Poetry,' he wrote, 'belongs to the common man, and expresses for him emotions that move within his own mind for which he can find no adequate release in his own thought or speech.' His ambition,

then, in his dialect poems, was to create a local tradition within
the larger national tradition that would express the feelings of
ordinary Orcadians. His aims are achieved in his best work
when his sense of the austere timelessness of the Greek lyric and
Orkney meet.

> *Thine are we evermore, O Crucified!*
> *Thine are we evermore, and on Thy side.*
>
> 'Thine Evermore'

The publication of his poems opened up a new world for
Rendall. He did some poetry reviewing for *The Glasgow Herald*,
and he met fellow poets such as Edwin Muir and Douglas
Young. He began working on an anthology of Scottish sonnets,
and in the introductory essay he mapped out the Scottish
literary tradition as he saw it. He felt Scottish poetry had
depended too closely on untutored inspiration, 'ae spark o'
Nature', and that this degenerated too easily into the banalities
of the Kailyard. In the essay, Rendall traced the academic
tradition in Scottish poetry—sonnet-writing provided a test of its
health—from the court-poets of James VI's reign through to the
contemporary 'academic scholar-poets'. He delighted in the
earlier poets' cosmopolitan awareness: 'It was not merely that
these had travelled widely, read deeply, and rubbed shoulders
with men in varied stations of life, but that they moved in a
common cultural world with Frenchmen, Spaniards, Italians,
and Englishmen, without ceasing to be Scotsmen.'

The loss of the court, he maintained in the essay, was the
greatest cultural disaster that Scotland had suffered, although
from 'the enduring root of the vernacular' eighteenth-century
poetry had sprung. Contemporary recovery would come, he
thought, when 'ae spark o' Nature' was combined with 'the
cultivated elegance of art'. 'The cure for "kailyairdism" lies,' he
wrote, 'not in extracolloquial speech, but in common idioms
more sensitively used.' He admired the view of the Classicist
which saw the individual taking from the tradition, thereby
avoiding eccentricity, and in turn contributing to the common
heritage. The position he was propounding, however, was
unfashionable; in addition the essay was written with a certain
stiffness of movement. 'A Book of Scottish Sonnets' failed to

find a publisher and Rendall, partly under the pressure of other activities, did not further develop his writing on literary subjects.

George Mackay Brown has recalled how the climate of the post-war years in Orkney was favourable for literature. A few days after his review of *Country Sonnets* had appeared, Rendall had written to him, and the two men established a friendship. This was to flourish when Rendall became a frequent visitor during a spell in hospital in 1953-4. After the death of James Tulloch, Rendall's closest friend was Ernest Marwick, the future folklorist of Orkney and Shetland, then a young bookshop assistant in Kirkwall. In modern times literary activity in Orkney had largely been channelled into historical writing, and the islands had produced little in the way of poetry. But this now began to change. In the earlier part of the twentieth century there had been a revival of interest in the islands' cultural links with Scandinavia, and a society had been formed to study and foster them. But the first of the new Orcadian writers, Edwin Muir and Eric Linklater, were part of the Scottish Literary Renaissance of the twenties and thirties. Linklater's novels set in the islands had expanded imaginative horizons, and as Muir's poetry appeared Robert Rendall, Ernest Marwick and George Mackay Brown keenly discussed it. Ernest Marwick provided a context for this activity with his *Anthology of Orkney Verse,* which rigorously excluded the sentimental and gathered the poetry of the islands from the Norse period until modern times. It appeared in 1949 while Rendall was working on his Orkney variants and his Scottish sonnet anthology. And in 1954 George Mackay Brown published *The Storm,* his first book of poetry.

Rendall and Brown were lyric poets. They shared an appreciation of Classical poetry, and they both took Orkney as their subject. But they were aware of contrasts in their work. George Mackay Brown gave voice to their differences in perspective in 'Sonnet', a poem dedicated to Robert Rendall:

> You have been here, before your latest birth,
> (Cheeks, at the pan-pipes, apple red and round!)
> Followed your wooden plough through Attic earth,
> And pulled your lobsters from a wine-dark sound.

> Now for a flicker of time you walk once more
>   In other islands, under geese-grey skies,
> And note, on Birsay hill and Birsay shore,
>   The year's glad cycle out of ancient eyes.
>
> O happy grove of poetry! where the soul
>   Is never sundered from the laughing blood,
> But sweetly bound, harmonious and whole,
>   In covenant with animal and god.
>
> But I came here unheralded, and meet
>   Angels and demons walking on the street.

The poem anticipates Brown's mature idiom, but he has not included it in any of his collections. Rendall, naturally, was delighted with it. Writing in 1955 to his nephew, Bert Rendall, he provided a commentary on it:

> About that poem of GMB dedicated to me, I really feel proud of it as a piece of work. You will doubtless have noted that the first quatrain has *the isles of Greece* & its poetry in mind: "pan-pipes" "wine-dark" sea (Homer's phrase) & that having been there in the remote past I have had a recent reincarnation in *the Orkney isles*!!! A poet's fantasy! The last two lines that elude you refer, of course, to GMB's (Islandman's) tempestuous style of writing in contrast to my placid contentment! The sonnet (as a poem) is a fine piece of work.

Rendall was forty-eight when *Country Sonnets* appeared, and although by the nineteen-fifties his most creative period as a poet was behind him, it was in this decade that he produced most of his books. In this flow of activity it is difficult to remember that he still earned his living as a draper, though by now he was a partner in the business, which gave him a certain freedom of action. He was quick and energetic in his movements but he found the process of composition a slow one. He had a hexagonal summer house in his garden in Willow Road, Kirkwall, and it was there he did much of his later writing. Ernest Marwick lived nearby and, when working on a poem, Rendall would run across the little copse that separated their houses several times a day to discuss its progress.

From childhood Rendall had suffered from occasional attacks of neurasthenia, brought on especially through overwork, and this taught him the necessity of being able to relax. He was a keen trout fisher and he kept boats on the Loch of Boardhouse and the Loch of Wasdale, proud that this linked him with his fishermen ancestors. Painting, his other means of relaxation, although pursued with the usual enthusiasm, was never a great success and he was actually a rather better photographer, another of his hobbies for a while. He had acquired a small cottage on the shore in Birsay, and it was to this that he would escape on holidays and at the occasional weekend to recuperate.

His mother died in 1949. During her final years she had needed almost constant care and he had had to give up Northbank. He never married and now, no longer tied to home, he used the summer months for travelling. He visited friends and relatives on the British mainland and he toured museums and art galleries and exhibitions. He began to visit Europe once more—although his increasing deafness added to the difficulties of travelling. He visited Germany, France and Switzerland again; but it was Italy in particular which drew him this time. He had read all his life of Italian Renaissance art, and seeing it was the fulfilment of an ambition. He became especially attached to Pesaro, an Adriatic seaport of fishermen and modern business people. He called it 'my hometown in Italy' and it provided a base for his travels in Italy during the nine visits he made—often staying for several weeks at a time—until 1964.

Again it was largely his interest in missionary work that had taken him to Italy initially, and he became close friends with the English missionaries in Pesaro, Tom and Beatrice Harding. He accompanied them in their trips into the hills near Pesaro and joined in their services, speaking in his halting Italian to the children or in translation to the adults. The lay leadership of the Brethren means that the members are closely involved in their church's affairs. Rendall had done lay preaching all his life, and for a number of years he had written for religious magazines. His next two books grew out of this writing. The first of these was *History, Prophecy and God* (1954), a study of the relationship between divine promise and historical fulfilment in the Bible. This theme enabled him to consider the mysteries of human existence that Christianity claims to answer. In the introduction he wrote:

Archaeology has opened up our horizons and demonstrated with conspicuous realism the continuity of civilization. By way of cultures now dead and buried the living present is linked with the remote past. Is there, then, within and above this extraordinary natural development, now covering a period of several millennia, a single directive Will, governing the course of human affairs? If so, it follows that upon our knowledge of this ultimate basis of history hangs a secure and contented attitude to life.

It was in the context of this problem that he set out in the book to examine the unity of scripture's predictive element and its outworking in biblical history. It was, as F. F. Bruce pointed out in his foreword, a theme that had been recently examined by academic theologians. In his own investigation Rendall was attempting to establish the Christian interpretation of history.

History, Prophecy and God was a serious attempt at constructing a history of salvation, but his next book, *The Greatness and Glory of Christ* (1956), while obviously the work of someone who read the Bible closely, was less technically theological and was weighted towards the devotional. In theology Rendall was a follower of the apostle Paul, who made Christ the centre of his thought. It was through Christ, Rendall held, that God achieved reconciliation, and subjection to Christ was the goal to which all things moved. He was the pattern for the Christian life: reconciliation should be the keynote in relations among Christians, and the spirit of self-sacrifice should inform living. In *History, Prophecy and God* Rendall saw the death and resurrection of Christ as the decisive crisis in human history. 'What is Scripture itself,' he now asked in the new book, 'but the record, first, of the tragic story how sin brought estrangement between God and man, but also of the reconciling action of God in Christ, whereby man is restored into fellowship with his Creator, and his fellow-men?' His theological writings show an occupation with this large vision, coupled with a close attention to the detail of the text of the Bible.

Some of the stricter groups of Christian Brethren have gained an unenviable reputation for narrowness. The parents of Rendall's close contemporary, the Scottish poet William Montgomerie, were Brethren members in Glasgow, and in his poems about his childhood Montgomerie presents the church as being stifling and constricted. But the congregation that Montgomerie was brought up in later seceded from the parent body to join a yet stricter group. Rendall, however, remained committed to the Brethren form of church, despite offers from two different denominations of a theological education and a pastoral charge. He belonged to the mainstream body, by far the largest of Brethren groups, sometimes called 'Open Brethren' to distinguish them from the more exclusive Brethren churches. He practised the ecumenicity which was the intention of most of the pioneers, while deploring the fissiparous tendencies of the stricter groups. Rendall was also convinced that human culture was a gift of God's grace for life's enrichment. Although most Brethren had been antipathetic to cultural involvement, there had always been others such as Charles Smith, Rendall's mentor in the Kirkwall Brethren, who wrote verse and had been President of the Kirkwall Literary and Debating Society. After he had been to a service in a Kirkwall church at which the twenty-third Psalm had been sung, Rendall wrote in a letter to Ernest Marwick: ' "goodness and mercy" takes in, among other things, painting and poetry.'

There was, nevertheless, the potential for tension. His type of Christianity could not be peripheral to life, but his interests had to be integrated with it. Rendall's faith, though secure, was not complacent and so he had investigated the challenges to it. He felt that to depict Scottish religious life as being all gloom, an image that was popular with contemporary writers (and which Rendall called 'the Calvin myth'), was to ignore its other aspects. He concluded, in the words of one of his poetry reviews, that 'the Christian faith itself, so far from being an outmoded 'enamilit tale', has shown a power of survival in human hearts for almost 2000 years that forbids us to think that it will succumb to the intellectual caprices of the twentieth century.'

Again Orkney helped in this resolution. During Robert Rendall's lifetime, most of the islands' intellectual leaders had a significant church connection. He had been given an appreciation of older forms of Scottish Christianity through his attendance at the Original Secession Church in Birsay (known locally as 'the Kirk abune the Hill'), where many of his closest friends worshipped. In addition, Evangelicalism was strong among the Orkney churches, having made an impact throughout the nineteenth century. From 1868 onwards, Brethren churches had been formed. In that year they had made their biggest impression in Westray, where Rendall's paternal family originated. Smaller congregations later came into existence in a number of places, along with the robust church in Kirkwall where Rendall was a member. And in Orkney generally, while religious adherence was weakening, values were still largely shaped by Christianity.

ORIGINAL SECESSION CHURCH, ABUNE-THE-HILL, BIRSAY

Even among those who were touched by Evangelicalism in early life but later rejected it, there could still be a residual effect. Edwin Muir, for example, born in Deerness in 1887, adopted in his youth the Evangelical piety of his parents. He later came to reject it before returning to the Christian faith—although not in any of its institutional forms. In 1964 Willa Muir wrote to Rendall, 'Edwin's Christianity (very real) extended more widely than the usual ecclesiastical Christianity, which he didn't much care for.' Muir's Orcadian childhood influences, however, can be seen behind his later religious faith. Rendall's Evangelicalism, then, was an additional point of contact with Orkney society.

In the Brethren too there were a number of scholarly figures, mainly in England, who were men of an unsectarian and independent spirit. Rendall's ability had been early recognised by individuals such as C. F. Hogg, an itinerant preacher among them; E. H. Broadbent, a church historian and missionary; and Professor F. F. Bruce, a noted New Testament scholar and fellow-Scot. He had received encouragement from them to develop his writing: it was due to Hogg's influence that he published his first article. His closest friend in this circle, however, was J. B. Watson, editor of the most important of the Brethren magazines, *The Witness*. Rendall often stayed in

43

London with Watson while passing to and from the continent, and Watson came north to Orkney on several occasions. Watson was also interested in painting, and the two men would visit the annual exhibition at the National Gallery in London together, while in Orkney Rendall introduced Watson to the mysteries of fishing. When Watson died in 1955 Rendall was asked to edit some of his uncollected writings and to preface them with a biography. *J. B. Watson: A Memoir and Selected Writings* appeared in 1957, and the following year he edited a small volume of Watson's religious essays.

It had long been a matter of regret to him that his religious poetry never matched his secular. But in *Shore Poems* (1957) he finally achieved two religious poems of worth. 'The Trial' manages a simple dignity that had hitherto eluded his religious poetry, while 'Thine Evermore' gives vigorous expression to the dedication he brought to his faith. It is perhaps significant in view of his difficulty in finding an adequate voice for his religious feeling that 'The Trial' is a hymn and 'Thine Evermore' is hymn-like in its tone. There were no dialect poems in this latest collection, but 'Renewal' represented his most successful sonnet in English. He regarded the disciplines of the sonnet as a test of a poet's abilities and he had attempted the form since his youth. In 'Renewal' he achieved the unfolding logic of the true sonnet. The desire to write poetry left him for long periods, and composition was often a tortured process: 'The Trial', for instance, had been written during the night between snatches of sleep and cups of tea. The subject of 'Renewal' is poetic inspiration—ironically it was written in one concentrated burst—and it brings to fine expression the mystery of its flowering and regret at its winter sleep:

> Ah would they uncoil
> Again from that inmost core, leaf, stem, flower, fruit.

Shore Poems, however, was in many ways a disappointment, for it did not represent an advance in his development as a poet; it was, nevertheless, a consolidation of his achievement.

In the scientific community he had become the recognised authority on the marine zoology of Orkney. He contributed regularly to *The Journal of Conchology,* and visiting researchers turned to him for help. Amidst the literary activity of the 1950s, he also brought his list of Orkney shell species to completion. It had been his original intention to combine it with an account of his own work, and through his reminiscences he hoped to encourage younger Orcadians to take an interest in natural science. But when Professor V. C. Wynne-Edwards of Aberdeen University was visiting Rendall and saw his shell collection and its catalogue, he immediately suggested that it should be published in a scientific journal. *Mollusca Orcadensia* was eventually read before the Royal Society of Edinburgh in 1955 and published in its proceedings. The publication of a scientific paper means that it has been vetted by the scientific community, and Rendall felt deeply honoured that his forty-year study of Orkney shell species should be brought to completion in this way. The following year, at Rendall's instigation, it was published as a separate book and thus made available to the Orkney public.

Mollusca Orcadensia summed up the work of previous Orcadian conchologists who had worked within the older theoretical framework of using the shell only as a guide to classification. Rendall tracked down their lists, sometimes through the marginal annotations of books from their libraries or in their contributions to museum collections, and he carefully collated them. This meant that he was able to give a historical dimension to the notes on species distribution. He was also aware of the more recent scientific interest in marine zonation and other ecological aspects of molluscs. He saw his work of cataloguing local species as establishing the 'grammar' of ecological studies, and thought that it would enable later scientists to progress to more significant work by helping them to chart changing oceanic conditions through the presence or absence of individual species. Particularly in the essay that prefaced the species list, he explored the ecological significance of his work. When he was later compared to Philip Gosse, the influential pioneer of Victorian marine zoology who was also a member of the Brethren, Rendall was greatly pleased.

The separate publication of *Mollusca Orcadensia* left him free to trace the interconnections of his life on the shores of Orkney in another book. It appeared in 1960, significantly called *Orkney Shore*. It is a mature book expressing the satisfaction of a full life, serene in its sense of the way his varied interests formed a whole. It begins with an account of his wonder, having recently left the restrictions of Glasgow, at nature's freedom in Orkney and his growing interest in the life of the shore. This occupation on the shore, though, was for him

45

a way of sharing in the life of those generations of Orcadians, the subjects of his best poetry, who had lived off it and whose lives had been moulded by it, for 'the unseen influences of the shore get into one's blood'. The strands were held together for him because he saw the shore and its life as evidence of God's creative ingenuity. As he studied microscopic molluscs or as he noticed the relationship between the creature and its shell, he felt that he was gaining an insight into the secrets of the Creator; behind the beauty of the shell, mathematical in its proportions, he saw an ideal beauty that existed in the mind of God. And the sea was an image of a bountiful providence:

> What is it that so moves us as we stand on the shore and look out over the ocean? Not thought alone, or even imagination, but natural response to an immensity and wealth of life exceeding our power to grasp . . . Its continual motion, its potential of storm and tempest, its remoteness and mystery, its primeval birth, all combine to cast an awe upon our spirits and to soothe the inborn restlessness of our hearts. There is healing in the sea for mind and body.

The quality of his prose at times makes this one of his most satisfying books. Ernest Marwick felt that it was *Orkney Shore,* along with *Orkney Variants,* which revealed Rendall best.

He produced one final slim book of poetry, *The Hidden Land* (1966). He never was a prolific poet and his gift was for the lyric, the briefest of forms. Although he had always wanted to write a long poem celebrating Orkney, his two longer dialect poems were not successful. But after the completion of *Mollusca Orcadensia* he found himself with time to appreciate the spiritual in nature again. The poet, he had come to believe, was the priest of nature, apprehending the original creative impulse and glimpsing the world as it was in its infancy in Eden; this vision he mediated to his audience. In this way Rendall was trying to link faith, which grasped the createdness of everything, with poetic insight, which grasped the inward reality behind the outward form. In a manner reminiscent of Wordsworth, he felt earth and cliffs and seas impressing themselves on the mind. His nature mysticism can be seen in poems like 'Autumn Sunset' and 'The Masque'. *The Hidden Land* is dedicated to Edwin Muir, and Muir's influence is present in the way Nature's pageant can momentarily reveal the innocent essence of things:

But I have seen, like treasure long concealed,
  A sudden radiance break from evening skies,
And everything on sea and shore and field
  In flawless essence move, without disguise . . .

But this poetry of nature is uneven in accomplishment; and
'The Floss, Westray', a vision of wholeness at the ruins of his
ancestral croft, gives more complete expression to the reality he
found hidden behind appearance. Always keen to experiment,
he also included some haikus, poems of seventeen syllables,
which he had discovered when a missionary had sent him some
examples from Japan. The economy of form and the brief
images were similar to some of the shorter lyrics (themselves
learned from the epigrams in *The Greek Anthology*) he had
written previously. It is one of these, 'Last Obsequies', which
George Mackay Brown has seen as uniting Rendall's life with
that of the Orkney crofter-fisherman. 'With this book,' he
wrote at the time in his review in *The Orcadian*, 'Mr Rendall
has arrived at a station of light and tranquillity.'

  Hands on gunwale — to the noust
  haul this weathered yawl:
    there leave her, safely housed.

'Last Obsequies'

He had retired from business in 1963, and this had left him
free to pursue his painting and fishing and to travel south in the
summer. But in 1965 his health broke, and the following year
after a period in hospital in Aberdeen during a serious illness, he
settled in St Peter's Home, Stromness, a home for the elderly. In
Stromness his friendship with George Mackay Brown was
resumed. He also made friends with Ian MacInnes, a Stromness
artist and art teacher. He found a new enthusiasm in Ian
MacInnes's painting and he had his portrait painted by him. He
grew fond of the town and it was in the museum there, with its
tradition in natural history, that his shell collection was
eventually deposited. He was gratified by the honours that came
his way: two of his poems, 'The Planticru' and 'Shore Tullye',
were included in *The Oxford Book of Scottish Verse* (1967), and
that same year the Queen awarded him a pension on the Civil
List for services to literature. Later he was to become one of the

few Scottish poets included by Philip Larkin in *The Oxford Book of Twentieth Century English Verse* (1973) when Larkin chose his 'Angle of Vision' for the anthology.

Edwin Muir had encouraged him to write an autobiography and he had made a start on this enterprise in 1952, but it had been laid aside under the pressure of other activities of the 1950s. He returned to the idea now but it was never to be written. Early in 1967 his health deteriorated and he was taken into hospital in Kirkwall. During his stay there he produced two final pieces of writing that reflected on his life. It is to this period that his history of the Orkney Antiquarian Society belongs. Fittingly, this, his last prose work of length, was about the Society that had nurtured Orkney's cultural life—and his own—in the inter-war years. And a fortnight before his death, completely deaf and hardly able to write, he dictated his last poem, 'On a London Street', to Ernest Marwick and George Mackay Brown. It recalled an incident that he had seen in London in the thirties, when he had met some young slum children returning from the fields carrying wild flowers. The poem is a brief metaphor of his life; for the children had escaped the miseries of industrialism to glimpse the glory of God in creation.

He died on 8th June, 1967. On the Tuesday following his death, Sheriff D. B. Keith took the unusual step of paying tribute to him before the court began its business. 'In the judgement of many,' he said, 'Robert Rendall was the most outstanding man of his time reared and brought up in these islands.' This esteem was echoed by others in Orkney from their different perspectives. John Oddie, a close friend in the Kirkwall Brethren, spoke at the funeral of the enrichment Robert Rendall had brought: 'We are the better for having known such a man,' he said simply. In the following year, Ernest Marwick said in a radio broadcast, 'He will become a legend in our islands as the years go on, as stories about him are remembered, as his achievement is more widely recognised.' In 1969 George Mackay Brown published an affectionate essay on him in *An Orkney Tapestry*, recalling his memories of their friendship and assessing Rendall's achievement as a poet who at his best wrote 'marvellous lyrics, in the Orkney dialect, with a Greek form and purity.'

A life, Robert Rendall believed—and particularly the life of a Christian—should be a work of art. To his achievements must be added his personal qualities. Rendall had a gift for companionship with a great range of people, from university professors to Orkney crofters. He was attentive to his friends: writing to them, visiting them and dedicating his books to them; his lively humour, seen in his letters, brought them laughter. He relished his interests and had an ability to inspire interest in others. 'You would find in Robert's home in Kirkwall, or in his summer house in Birsay,' Ernest Marwick recollected in his radio tribute, 'all kinds of natural objects. Forgotten in the bath, starfishes or an octopus would infect the surrounding air; but you were recompensed by glimpses of remarkable hydroids, seen under his powerful microscope.' He recalled meeting him in a cafe in a small Scottish town when Rendall had just returned from Italy. Full of his paintings, Rendall arranged a line of chairs and placed his sketches on them to illustrate where he had been. He stopped only when a waitress had to ask politely for the chairs back. Although he had moments of depression, especially when he had been over-working, his world was a supremely happy one.

In Rendall we see the interests of Orkney culture and society of his time in microcosm. There are perhaps other ways in which we might see Orkney reflected in him. George Mackay Brown has argued that the Orcadian unites in his character the imaginative and the practical; and Howie Firth has seen the blending of interests as an Orkney characteristic: 'To shine light from several angles to get better illumination is nothing new in the islands: the life of Robert Rendall, poet and scientist, would be a concrete example of the process.' Rendall's understanding of creation and culture was a Christian one, and he explored his Orcadian heritage in the freedom of his faith. He stands with the body of Orkney writers whose religious vision of life has led them to protest against the materialism of the twentieth century: the formation of an industrial society which depresses its inhabitants and which starves the human spirit. Against this Rendall celebrated the shores of Orkney where he found a people encircled by the infinite sea.

SELECTED LETTERS
OF
ROBERT RENDALL

TO PROFESSOR WILLIAM BARCLAY

William Barclay (1907-78) was a noted communicator of Christian doctrine who was well-known in Scotland for his popular Bible commentaries and devotional books. He was Professor of Divinity and Biblical Criticism at Glasgow University from 1963-74. His papers have not survived, and this draft copy of a letter is all that is left of the correspondence between him and Robert Rendall. It was evidently written about 1955 when Rendall was working on biblical prophecy and it concerns the Greek word for 'presence' (parousia) which in the New Testament represents the word used by Jesus of his Second Advent. But the letter begins with a recurring theme of Rendall's correspondence—the creative process.

[c1955]

[Dear Rev. Wm. Barclay,]

I like your recent "British Weekly" *leader* shall I call it? on 'taking time for things'.[1] Do you fish trout? I often go a-fishing on one of our Orkney lochs, and have come to take the experience as a symbol of life and of creative work. For a while one has to pull strenuously up the loch, it may be against a strong wind: it is all 'effort'. Then the delightful moment comes: the boat is put broadside on against the wind and the drift begins. All effort ceases. One merely casts a fly lightly on the water, not knowing what may follow, when lo, a trout rises, then another, and then another. The point is this, it is during the 'drift' that the trout are caught. I've always wanted to write a poem about this. How often in our studies we have toiled and strained our minds in an effort to gain a point of vantage for understanding some problem. Then, after an idle moment, when

53

the mind is relaxed, the trout begin to rise, and we get them, one after another (if we use the net quickly enough) into our basket. The trouble is, you might be in a tramcar, or at the dinner-table with company, and the choice is a frantic decision whether to jot down the idea furtively on a scrap of envelope, or try to fix it temporarily in the memory until an opportune time to write it down occurs.

I'm almost afraid to embark on a critical theological query, but I must ask you something about the Greek word 'parousia', the more so since I have followed what you have to tell us about the doctrine of 'the second coming'. Perhaps I can best do so by giving you a little of my own thinking over it. I was brought up, as you know, in the circle of the so-called 'open brethren'—where I still most happily belong. The views of prophecy among us are largely programmatic in their approach, and if you have read my HISTORY, PROPHECY & GOD (pp. 67-68) you will have perceived that I have come to have a strong antipathy to this mode of studying the theme. Yet there *ARE* great unmistakable landmarks, that not only have recurring 'fulfilments' throughout the course of time but are to have a grand climax at the end . . .

I'm aware (partly, at least) of your own attitude to prophetic questions, and share some of them. But even if we concede that the language of prophecy is largely couched in Jewish thought forms, the fulfilment of much of it takes place in actual history, even if the climax is beyond time, and therefore beyond history. I recognize, too, that heavenly realities (and events, if that is a proper word to use concerning a sphere in which 'time' has no meaning) can only be understood by us now in terms of earthly symbols and experience . . .

---

[1] William Barclay had his own page in *The British Weekly* for a number of years.

TO GEORGE MACKAY BROWN

George Mackay Brown (b.1921), the Orkney poet and writer, has established an international reputation. He published his first book of poems in 1954, and since then he has produced an impressive body of work including essays, short stories, novels and several more collections of poetry. He studied at Newbattle Abbey

*College in 1952-3 when Edwin Muir was Warden and, after a
period in hospital in Orkney, returned in 1957 to prepare for
entering Edinburgh University. Born in Stromness, the 'Hamnavoe'
of his fiction, he has lived there all his life apart from his periods of
study. The town itself and the islands of Orkney have been the
inspiration and subject of his writing. He first met Rendall after
reviewing* **Country Sonnets** *in 1946 and the two men established
a friendship having a love of literature and Orkney in common. At
this time they frequently discussed each other's work—the subject of
these letters. Since he first read Rendall's poetry, George Mackay
Brown has remained a persistent advocate of its merits.*

Kirkwall, 13 October 1947

Dear George,

A thousand thanks for sending down the Shakespeare!
When you next are down I shall settle up with you for the cost
of it. Though the paper is perhaps a bit yellower than it used to
be in this edition, one is thankful to get a copy at all, and we
have become so accustomed to deteriorating circumstances that
it may be in the future my present copy will appear startlingly
white in comparison to those produced then.

I shall indeed be grateful for a peep at Andrew Young's
latest book, since, as you know, I value nature poems when
they are well done. So that enchantment still awaits me. At
present I am 'immersed' in Walter de la Mare's "Collected
Poems". As a rule I do not care for "Collected Works", as one
only finds the favourites already known through the antholo-
gies, and the evident inferiority of the rest becomes tantalising.
But with this book I have come to realise how consistent Walter
de la Mare is, and how various.

Then on Saturday night I read for the first time "Murder in
the Cathedral", which impressed me tremendously, and even
gave me a sense of the Shakespearean. You are much better
acquainted with Eliot than I am.

Thanks, too, for sending me the copy of ELEGY: FOR
PHYRRA. It is one of those pieces that one sometimes likes to
return again to. Your Easter Song[1] raised a mild excitement in
my mind; it is so clear and spontaneous in its movement, quite
in the manner of the old carols, I thought, and (very slightly)
reminiscent of Francis Thompson, but nevertheless wholly your

own. I liked it immediately. At first I was slightly confused in the exact meaning of the second line of the first stanza. There is an ellipsis of course, but though your punctuation makes it clear enough when one looks again, at first sight the mind carries over the first line into the second and then after "anointed" the suddenness of the ellipsis seems to throw one (myself at any rate) off the balance. Would you consider having a comma after the first line, and the period after "anointed". "Shed His pain and loss?" would then have the brevity which admits of the effective use of an ellipsis. But this may be mere pedantry! The final line of the poem swings rapidly into its place. Some might think almost too much so, the words being so familiar (as to be robbed of their high meaning and their power also as an original IMAGE). I refrain from criticising this, as from experience I know only too well how, when a fit phrase like this comes in one's mind, it is difficult to think of any other. But I really like this poem.

The Dark Land I am not so sure of. The final section reads well, but I find it difficult to get the central idea behind the poem; this, however, may well be my stupidity! The two peats licking each other presents no difficulty to my mind. I saw the image at once before I read your explanation. But if you feel the difficulty is a real one, could you not substitute "stone hearth" for "stone floor"? The Epitaph reads neatly, but both the short pieces fall short, I think, of your later work. I showed them all to Ernest and to Mrs Marwick. They share my liking for the Easter piece. Ernest has his anthology complete now, I think, in all its details, so we hope that he will speedily find a publisher.

The exhibition of pictures in The Arts Club is excellent and well worth more than one visit. You will find them both satisfying and exciting, quite apart from their strong local interest.

Again with thanks for your kind service in procuring the copy of Shakespeare, and hoping to see you soon.

Yours very sincerely,
Robert Rendall

[1] In this letter Rendall is commenting on three early unpublished poems by George Mackay Brown, 'Easter Song', 'The Dark Land' and 'The Epitaph'.

Kirkwall, 8 April 1948

Dear George,

My immediate re-action on reading your poem[1] in the current issue of "The New Shetlander" was to say to myself, This is the genuine thing. The reaction was instinctive, and I do not think it will be much modified after re-reading. It is, I think, the best of your work that I have seen, mature both in thought and expression, has no crudities, is perfectly controlled throughout yet possesses fluidity. It has the requisite 'hardness' and tightness of expression without being stiff. You have projected yourself imaginatively into your subject, so that as a poem it doesn't matter tuppence whether Hakon really felt that way or not. I really think you've got off with it this time!

You will appreciate this all the more when I say that I do not share your leanings to a Catholic approach to religious experience, though I have a great admiration for certain of the early Fathers, and also have had genuine personal friendships with individual Catholics. But in this poem you have—in my judgment—entered convincingly into Hakon's mind, and given us a memorable imaginative reconstruction. The image of the "roosts of time" is not only most suited to the theme, but has that magnificent sweep about it that carries away the mind of the reader. I don't want to give you the impression that I have not read your poem critically—I'll do that yet! though I'm pretty confident that my original impression will remain—but it certainly "captured" me on the spot when I read it, and I am too fastidious and suspicious for that to happen very often.

You have a mind that takes imaginative flights, and when these, as in this poem, have *an actual historical incident* to flutter about in, they heighten that incident into poetic truth. But I find that to take such flights in fantasies out of one's own mind often results in indeterminate wanderings. Too often have I proved this in my own experience. It is a paradox that if we would soar to the clouds we must (to mix the metaphor) keep one foot firmly on the earth. Or is this a bad heresy?

Anyhow, I wanted to write and tell you of the pleasure that the reading of your poem gave me.

Yours very sincerely,
Robert Rendall

9.4.48
  P.S. I still like it today under a more sober scrutiny.
Congratulations!
                              R.R.

---

[1] 'Earl Hakon, on the Mediterranean, Sails Home for Orkney', *The New Shetlander*, No. 9 (1948). The poem is in the form of a soliloquy by Hakon, the killer of St Magnus, who is returning from pilgrimage to the Holy Land, having received the Church's pardon. Hakon sees "the dark roosts [*tidal races*, Orkney dialect] of time" sweeping round the event of Magnus's killing.

Kirkwall, 23 December 1949

My dear George,

   For a change I shall write you by hand: I always have an uneasy feeling about 'typing' personal letters, except on literary matters.

   First of all, congratulations on that excellent article you wrote recently under your pen-name for The Orcadian. Like myself Mr John Mooney thought highly of it. It read felicitously and the inevitability of the phrasing was delightful—the result, I suspect, of the art which hides art. And the article, too, had a restraint which added to its "judicious" style. Yes, George, you carried it off this time!

   Thanks, too, for "Ur"—his imagination must be very dulled indeed who can read of such archaeological adventures without a thrill of excitement.

   Then in the recent "New Shetlander" I liked your poem[1] written after the manner of Edwin Muir. You have affinities, and though this poem certainly recalls Edwin Muir at his best (or near best!) it is something to have done it so effectively: your own particular idiom will follow when you have explored the new country.

   My own muse has fled—I know not whether but one day I shall again see her peeping round the corner of some Birsay rock!

   These last few weeks I have been busy getting my bachelor establishment set in order & going over old papers etc. One of my friends has given me as a Christmas present—what do you think? An aspidistra!!! No. *NOT* Ernest! Shades of Victorianism! As if I were not already incurably Victorian.

Wishing you a very happy Christmas & hoping to see you when you are down our way.

Yours sincerely
Robert Rendall

---

[1] *The New Shetlander,* No. 19 (1949), 'The Exile'. This poem, which was later included in *The Storm* (1954), has expulsion from Eden as its theme.

Kirkwall, 5 August 1952

Dear George,

I really had written you a letter some weeks ago, still unposted! but with the dust up of these summer weeks—Danish Conference, Visitors, B.B.C. and so on—I have been heads and heels. The broadcasts are behind us now, so we can shove them in a pigeon-hole. I liked the *descriptive* part of the Rackwick broadcast,[1] and could endorse its spirit and accuracy, having lived there myself and seen the incredible colours with my own eyes. But I felt some of the stories (which I did not hear well) a bit long-drawn-out and tedisome. Like Ernest and myself you will be glad to get back to our normal way of life, trout-fishing and putting!

I was glad to see you that day at the Royal[2] with the Muirs, but the place was so crowded that with my deafness I was afraid to embark on prolonged conversation with you, though I felt that we could have a lot to talk over: you will be in Kirkwall again soon, I hope.

We had a grand time with Dr. and Mrs Muir, and seemed this year to settle down with them to really easy conversations on all sorts of topics. They are both delightful people. Of course I saw a good deal of them also at the Conference, but one morning we spent the whole forenoon round the fireside in my living-room discussing things in easy fashion.

His new Collected Poems are delightful, and one becomes so fascinated with the poems themselves that one forgets that thin yellow paper on which they are printed. His New Poems are a sheer delight to read, and indicate that he is *even yet* growing in stature and that he has not reached the summit of his poetic achievement.

With the stimulus of recent weeks I have written a new

poem which seems to have excited Edwin; you must see it when you come down. It makes me myself feel as if I had written nothing hitherto, and my only alarm is that it may be an isolated trickle not to be followed by others in the same vein.

I have decided to publish my anthology of Scottish Sonnets this winter, at the Orcadian Office, a limited edition. I discussed the matter with Dr Muir who encourages me to this resolve already made by myself.[3] Then a London publisher is interested in a theological study on HISTORY, PROPHECY AND GOD which I began many years ago, and now must try to complete. You would probably disagree with parts of it, but I think that it would 'interest' you. Beyond that I have a score of literary commitments. The Shell Book has been postponed for a bit, though I am still working at times on the material. When the "Kathleen" was north they dredged some interesting material for me which I have gone over but not fully worked through.[4]

THEM AT ISBISTER recorded well for Ernest's script.[5] Harald Mooney read it well, and being himself a minister gave a touch of mischief to it. Ernest gave me a read of your ORKNEYMEN, some of which are wickedly well done! With a few pencil strokes you have them caught on paper, even if only in profile. Possibly you may have a future for this sort of sharp characterisation. I liked the last line of the Doctor with its recognition of his human quality of sympathy. I think that the note of compassion for human frailty might in one or two instances have been added in a similar way to the more keenly satiric of the others. Instead of diminishing the effect it would add '*understanding*' and 'pathos' and so heighten the general effect of the individual poems. But I am a poor critic, and you will have to follow your own daemon.

I hope that you get a few days of real Orkney summer before you leave for the south. I understand that you are likely to have another year at Newbattle. Congratulations!

Well, George, I must away down to the shop: I do not say, to WORK!

Hoping to see you soon
Robert

---

[1] 'Inheritance of Sea and Soil', a radio programme transmitted on 23 July, 1952 about Rackwick, Hoy, written by George Mackay Brown and Archie P. Lee to mark the Danish-Orcadian Conference in Kirkwall. The programme's title is a phrase from Rendall's poem 'The Planticru'.

[2] The Royal Hotel, Kirkwall.

[3] Despite this, the book was not published.

[4] The Fishery Research Vessel *Kathleen* dredged material for Rendall in deep water. He sifted the material for specimens.

[5] Ernest Marwick had compiled a programme on Orkney poetry entitled 'The Orcadian at Home' for the radio series 'Chapbook'. It was transmitted on 1 February, 1953. It included poetry by David Vedder, Duncan Robertson, Robert Rendall, Christina Costie, and George Mackay Brown. 'Them at Isbister' by George Mackay Brown was published as the last in a series of seven poems entitled 'Orcadians' in *The Storm* (1954). 'Doctor' was the fifth poem. The published version of the poems has been revised.

TO STANLEY CURSITER

In the course of a distinguished career, the artist Stanley Cursiter (1887-1976) was Director of the National Galleries of Scotland 1930-48, and the Queen's Painter and Limner for Scotland. As an artist he was best known for his landscapes and portraits. He was born in Kirkwall, and the Orkney landscape was the inspiration in much of his best work. Robert Rendall admired his work and he collected several of his paintings. The two men corresponded regularly after the publication of **Country Sonnets**. *They had in common a love of the arts and of exploring the Orkney shoreline and countryside. Cursiter stayed in Stromness during the summer and most of the letters were written in winter.*

Kirkwall, 23 December 1949

Dear Mr Cursiter,

I have not had a card printed this Christmas but I wish to return the kind greeting sent by Mrs Cursiter and yourself and to wish you both a very happy Christmas.

My first gift from Santa Claus this year was your "Scottish Art" which I shall now be able to re-read at greater leisure. I must ask you to autograph it for me—if you have no objection—as you did my "Peploe".[1]

My next gift was a six-leaved specimen of the much maligned 'aspidistra' for my Victorian room! sent by a

61

E

discerning friend! It will go with the rocking-chair and photograph albums.

I read with very great interest the account of your talk on "Stromness" and feel glad to think that you have found a community in Orkney that seem responsive to the preservation of our local architecture and willing to consider its extension on traditional lines. I fear that in Kirkwall we have got into a muddle over divided counsels and that "the preservers" are losing heart. Shore Street is a standing monument to lost opportunities and is neither ancient nor modern. A deliberate attempt at confusion could not have been more successful. Victoria Street is gradually being 'improved' likewise. Some years ago there was a 'Save Victoria Street' movement but—first the causey went, then the old archway at the Royal Hotel Close, now the old houses are going—one by one—and soon it seems we shall have a gradual replacement by what the late William Traill was disposed to call "warts". I seriously doubt whether the old houses at the top of Broad Street will be pre-served *even in part*. Will they be replaced by a building glaringly modern or by an even worse atrocity—an imitation antique?

But I must not become a 'grumbler': after all, we Kirkwallians shall always be able to take the bus and see how well things can be done in Stromness. May your plans and friendly counsel take effect there!

It seems likely that during 1950 I shall be able to take an extended trip abroad—perhaps for two or three months—to visit friends in various countries. If so I am planning to see one or two Italian towns—Pisa & Florence at any rate, if not others. So that the poor trout at Boardhouse and elsewhere will heave a sigh of relief when they hear the news.

The other day I received a book of poetry from a Swedish poet who was here in the summer. That I cannot understand them makes, as you know, little difference if we are to accept modern canons. Ronald Mooney, who knows Swedish, is to attempt a review & perhaps a paraphrase or two of the poems. Mr Bodin has also written an article on "Stromness" which is to be translated and, in due course, printed in the Orcadian.

With best wishes for 1950

Yours sincerely
Robert Rendall

P.S. I know a good straw-back chair maker near Kirkwall. A Papey man, capable, too, of teaching!

[1] Stanley Cursiter, *Scottish Art to the Close of the Nineteenth Century* (1949), and *Peploe, An Intimate Memoir* (1947).

ALBERT STREET, KIRKWALL c.1920

Kirkwall, 3 August 1950

Dear Mr Cursiter,

. . . My first adventure was in Edinburgh where I acquired one of your paintings! I happened to be in Aitken & Dotts and, as is my custom, had a look upstairs. What did I see but an oil-painting of the West coast—with cliff-top in foreground, looking down toward a headland and the Hoy hills. I liked it immediately and though I should have valued your judgment in the selection of a picture, I decided that if I passed this

63

particular one by I should have a nagging regret for the rest of my life, since the view so completely epitomises how I see the Western coastline. Also I liked the painting with its economy of paint and colour. And besides, the picture itself will not overpower everything else in my humble home, though of course it will add distinction to the room . . .

My month in Italy was most memorable: twice I crossed the Apennines by car, and therefore saw a good deal of genuine peasant country. Florence fulfilled the desires of my boyhood and did not disappoint me. I lived with an Italian family just below Fiesole, right at the tramway terminus, so that it was easy either to run into the town or to turn to the country. Pisa, Urbino, Arezzo, Perugia, Pesaro, among other cities visited, each had their own attraction. But I saw nothing which gave that deep sense of absolute satisfaction and contentment which I always find up in Birsay! Nevertheless the wealth of experience gathered in such a trip makes it well worth while taking.

Wherever I went there seemed to be special exhibitions of paintings to visit as well as permanent collections. In Thun I saw work by Fred Hopf and Paul A. Wenger, mostly oils, though there were also a few water-colours. I found the Gallery at Basel extremely interesting, especially on the modern side: Hodler and Segantini, of course, drew my attention, but there were others also. At Bad Homburg the artists of the Taunus had staged a show which contained some memorable work, and also had some plastics. I found the Royal Academy exhibition in London very disappointing, except for the water-colours: to me the Scottish exhibition showed much more imagination and adventure. One could not escape the impression that many of the paintings, if not flat and dull, were mere tricks obviously straining after a novel effect . . .

To come north to Kirkwall and find a show here was exciting, and I find myself able to look at the pictures with a fresh eye. I like your picture of Stromness, of course, mainly because of the sparing way in which the paint is laid on—a change from the heavy daubs of much modern painting done in pure imitation of Van Gogh etc.—and also because of that peculiar over-all 'haze' which so many of your (recent?) paintings show: the restricted range of tones (or what appears to me to be *that*) produces to my mind not only a feeling of atmosphere characteristic of Orkney but a sense of the numinous in nature that most sensitive people feel . . .

Orkney, 4th July 1953

Dear Mr Cursiter,

Kirkwall has not been quite the same this summer without your occasional appearance on the street. Even letters in the paper are not quite the same as the friendly smile in passing!

We have had some delightful out-of-door's weather and by good fortune I have been able to take full advantage of it this year. In March I spent a week in Stronsay doing some shell collecting and pretty well walked round the island. It was the time of spout-ebbs[1] so I joined the local fraternity in this sport. Last month I had two weeks in North Ronaldshay—a memorable experience, though I spent the time lazily enough and for my amusement did eight oil-sketches. The meadows there are full of colour.

Early this year Dr A. P. Orr of the Marine Biological Station at Millport had a Robertson bucket-dredge made for me by their blacksmith and this promises to give good results in our Orkney waters. I have secured the willing & enthusiastic co-operation of one of our local fishermen in working it & already have had material from the haddock ground west of Rousay & also some stuff from the sand near Copinsay. I am re-forming my shell-collection in conjunction with the preparation of a catalogue of our Orkney mollusca and making steady though slow progress.

We have read with interest of your ploys in Edinburgh & feel honoured that one of Orkney's sons should have been given such a commission.[2] But your real reward in painting must come from your fellow-islanders' appreciation of your work. More and more I come to see the rewarding element in fulfilling one's life-tasks in the heart of a small integrated community. Were it not for the stimulus provided by visits to Art Galleries & the information gained by inspection of specimens in museums and (now), in a lesser degree, poking about in book-shops, I should have little inclination to leave Orkney . . .

---

[1] 'Spout' (pronounced 'spoot') is the Orkney name for the Razor-shell, a mollusc (*Solenidae* family). It betrays its presence in the sand by emitting a spout of water. At very low ebb-tides they are caught by walking backwards, watching for the spout, then deftly flicking them out of the sand. At one time a popular food-source, in *Mollusca Orcadensia* (pp. 191-2) Rendall cites a report of an occasion in 1861 when there were 100 people at the Sands of Ness (in St Andrews, Orkney) catching spouts.

[2] Stanley Cursiter had been commissioned to paint a portrait of the Queen.

Kirkwall, 11 September 1956

Dear Mr Cursiter,

This is something to add to your shelf of Orkney books.[1] It is, as you will see, bare bones, but it gives a pattern of our native molluscan fauna. It will be 40 years come the 15th Oct. since first I set myself to this task and it is a great satisfaction now to have brought it to a measure of completion. Originally I had intended to have clothed the skeleton with tissue and flesh, but Prof. Wynne-Edwards persuaded me to extract the bones and give them to science—so now I have been left with lumps of meat which I shall have to cook into some sort of dish for our Orkney readers. This will consist of reminiscences of our own earlier naturalists and of personal experiences in shore collecting, jellied into some single literary pattern. It will be an interesting experiment in writing.

The Fishery Research Vessel "Kathleen" is north again, with Dr Thomas from Aberdeen in charge of the scientific side. He is doing some special research work on lobsters, but also collecting hydrographical data for more general studies. Dr Lucas has again very kindly added to the programme of work the bringing of dredged material to me for detailed examination for invertebrates, so that I hope to have some interesting stuff to examine during the early months of winter.

Have you been able to do *any* painting this summer? Though there has not been much sun there must have been characteristic Orkney weather effects. I haven't touched a brush for over a year, but I still delight in looking at pictures.

With kindest regards to Mrs Cursiter & yourself

Yours sincerely
Robert Rendall

[1] A copy of *Mollusca Orcadensia*.

Kirkwall, 22 March 1957

Dear Mr Cursiter,

I saw Dr. Marwick[1] for a few minutes this morning, and he showed me what in pleasantry he called 'the rags'—and red ones at that. He mentioned also that you were now in your northern fastness again.

The way in which all classes of folk in our little community have responded to the idea of the Presentation Portrait has given those of us immediately concerned with it complete assurance that we have interpreted aright public feeling in the matter. There has been a warmth in the response that is highly gratifying.

The primary idea in our own minds was that of maintaining a worthy & imaginative local school tradition and now this purpose will have secured a *double* fulfilment in yourself and Dr Marwick. We feel ourselves extremely fortunate that you should have been willing to accept the commission and for making it possible by your generous co-operation.

About the end of next month I hope to spend 8 days in Paris with my nephew—by way of celebrating (as we hope) his taking of a Degree in Civil Engineering. I then go on for two weeks or so to the Adriatic—to collect a few more sea-shells and feel the kindly warmth of Italian sunshine again. I intend having a whole day in Ravenna to see the interiors of the Byzantine churches there—and perchance to drop a tear on Dante's grave.

I've had a return to verse this winter—a field that I have left fallow for a few years: I now look forward to ploughing up my leas,[2] and who can tell, perhaps even breaking up some fresh hill-ground. I've been greatly taken lately with some of the older Italian verse forms in cantos and stanziac patterns, and must explore and experiment with these—between trout fishing and business.

Your book on life in ancient Greece is safe and clean in my desk. I must return it to you one of these days.

With my best respects to Mrs Cursiter & yourself

Yours sincerely
Robert Rendall

---

[1] Dr Hugh Marwick (1881-1965), linguist and historian, was Rector of Kirkwall Grammar and then Director of Education for Orkney. Harald Mooney, Robert Rendall and John Shearer had raised a subscription from among his former pupils to have his portrait painted by Stanley Cursiter. Marwick was wearing his doctoral gown.

[2] *leas*: fallow ground.

HARBOUR, PESARO   12·5·57

Pesaro, Thursday, 15th [1957]

Dear Mr Cursiter,

When in Paris I visited the 170th exhibition of the Salon staged by the "Societé des Artistes Francais et des Beaux Arts de la France d'Outre-mer". To me it was a wonderful experience. The sculpture work was to my untutored eye excellent. The method of display of the paintings made seeing them very easy. There were very few portraits but these, first-class. The gold medal in this class was given to a painting of a Scottish Highlander in full dress! The absence of 'abstract' pictures took my notice: but there were plenty of these in the side streets near our hotel.

One day we went to Barbizon—a very satisfying day. I like Millet's pencil drawings—and his small pen & ink sketches.

One can easily see how Paris stimulates artists. There is such a movement of life and ideas in the pictures that art seems 'alive' there even if it goes into fantastic by-ways. My own impressions of what I saw made my mind alternate between despair of ever holding a pencil or paint-brush in my hand again—and a foolishly optimistic assurance that I would blossom into some wonderful masterpiece! Paris certainly creates illusions in the mind!

Last Monday my friends took me by car to Ravenna, where we saw several of the 6th cent. Churches (including San Vitale & both the Apollinare churches), the two Baptistries and one or two Roman tombs. I duly deposited my tribute of 3 Birsay grottie-buckies[1] at Dante's tomb!

The sunshine has been brilliant these last two days: I must get out now & finish one or two pencil sketches that I began the other day—street scenes, which always fascinate me. I've collected a few more shells from the Adriatic shore, but here in Pesaro I mostly idle about in the markets and among the folk.

With kindest regards to Mrs Cursiter & yourself

Yours sincerely
Robert Rendall

---

[1] A shell, the European Cowry (*Trivia monacha*)

Kirkwall, 10 January 1959

Dear Mr Cursiter,

Orkney is mantled in white: the sun on the snow is giving us an eerie light indoors. It is one of those days that give variety to the winter. Earlier this week I was up in Birsay for three days—a sort of New Year ritual. The weather was crisp & clear so that I spent a good deal of my time along the shore & out along the north cliffs. You always come into my mind at 'the whale's jaws': we have run across one another several times there.

Willie Harvey was out in his boat one afternoon & came in with 19 score: a score sheet, I told him, of the number I had boasted about him in my poem "Happy Fisherman". By some misunderstanding I missed being out with him—and in this frosty weather, cuithes do not 'take' near the rocks . . .

On the way up by bus last Monday—just as we were passing Wideford Hill in the darkening a poem began to unwind itself in my mind & two complete stanzas formed themselves completely *before* I reached Birsay. I was delighted, as it is over a year since the impulse to write in verse came upon me. A whole poem of seven stanzas is the result: perhaps you'll read it some day.

My hands have been idle with the paint-brush but one of these evenings I must recapture the delight of using paint on canvas. I do it mostly because I like to do so, and am more content with the doing than with my feeble results.

When in Parma I visited the Art Gallery where I saw an interesting Murillo & a fine head by Da Vinci. I added one or two specimens to my collection of Adriatic shells.

We miss you in Orkney but I hear that both Mrs Cursiter and yourself are in good health & enjoying what Edinburgh has to offer.

With sincere regards
Robert Rendall

[*Christmas card, December 1960*]

. . . Just now I'm deep in Hansell's biography of Edward Marsh—have you read it? 732 pages. An amazingly interesting book especially for those whose literary sympathies are conditioned by the pre-1914 outlook on life and writing. It's a long time since I've been so fascinated by a memoir. Dr M. and the Sheriff,[1] too, have been captivated by it . . .

[1] David B. Keith (1891-1979), Sheriff of Orkney.

Kirkwall, 17 December 1960

Dear Dr Cursiter,[1]

I applaud your decision to address me simply as 'Robert'. But respect due to years makes me retain the more formal in reply.

May I say how much encouraged I am by your kind reception of *Orkney Shore,* to which our Orkney public has given a welcome—if sales are any index. Now that the book is irrevocably in print I can think of several ways in which it might have been improved—and of items that might have been included. But it is out now just as it is.

This off my mind—I am turning my face in a fresh direction and would like to attempt something on the ecology of the exposed reefs along the North Shore of Birsay—which you are so familiar with and fond of. Although I have ranged over most of our shores I now feel that—so far—I have only been learning *the alphabet* on marine zoology & would now like to spell out a word or two—or even write a sentence, so to speak . . . It is most kind of you to have spoken to George Bruce[2] and I shall await developments with interest. Yes—we ought to be concerned with what can be fostered within Scotland itself (and in Orkney!!). I am, as you may already have guessed, a confirmed provincial . . .

[1] Stanley Cursiter had been given an honorary LL.D. by Aberdeen University.
[2] Stanley Cursiter had approached George Bruce, then an arts producer with the BBC, about the possibility of making a programme based around *Orkney Shore*. The programme was broadcast on 27th May 1962 with selections from, among others, the writings of George Mackay Brown, Eric Linklater, Edwin Muir and Robert Rendall (see letter to Stanley Cursiter of 7.5.62).

Kirkwall, 8 November 1961

Dear Dr Cursiter,

Winter has set in upon us with a vengeance. Since you left us weather has not allowed much painting out-of-doors, and other interests have crowded in to hinder anything being done in the house . . .

A few weeks ago a missionary friend from Japan, knowing my interest in verse, sent me a small anthology of Japanese in the Haiku tradition. This tightly constructed verse form (which has only 17 syllables arranged in 5/7/5 lines and is governed by a complex series of rules like our sonnet) has greatly fascinated me, and the attempt to use the form in English verse has become with me almost a disease. The economy of words (comparable with economy of line in Japanese pen-and-ink drawing and power of suggestion) makes a grand discipline. Everything must be pictorial, objective, elliptical, express a mood, time and season, have double or even triple images—but enough, I must send you a few samples to see what you make of them—and to know if you like them—and if so, which?[1] You have, I know, decided tastes in verse.

My stereoscopic binocular microscope came a few weeks ago, and I am now trying my prentice hand at slide making, which is a delicate operation. I hope to mount a series of Orkney hydroids, a branch of marine life that has fascinated me ever since boyhood but that hitherto I have been unable to follow up. Now, with my microscope I shall be able to study them more efficiently. I have been going through my text-books on marine life and extracting records other than those I have already listed in my ORKNEY SHORE, and have been surprised at what I have found—sponges, corallines, hydroids, etc., all the lower forms of the marine invertebrates. In the course of doing this I have come across other tracks of the elusive Lieut. Thomas, who did so much in recording marine forms in Orkney during the middle of the nineteenth century . . .

Please excuse my having done this in type-writing rather than by hand. I have become lazy at using the pen.

With my best respects to Mrs Cursiter and yourself,

Yours sincerely
Robert Rendall

[1] Several of Rendall's haikus were enclosed with the letter.

Kirkwall, 7 May 1962

Dear Dr Cursiter,

Trout have a way of "rising" unexpectedly so that the surfacing of your idea for a wee programme on our Orkney shore is not altogether strange. I appreciate your kind interest in the matter. The theme itself—which is the really important thing—should give excellent scope to the imagination of the producer . . .

Last Saturday afternoon I had the delightful privilege of conducting a party of the Orkney Field Club over on the exposed reefs on the north shore at Birsay—pointing out its pattern of sea-shore life. There were six carloads of us—& half the company were children up to "teenagers". These showed exceptional interest & were sharp-witted in their observations. I had taken a sea-weed press with me—it greatly attracted them & should lead to new ideas in their minds. It was a delightful afternoon.

The news of your impending arrival surely means that summer weather is at hand.

With kind regards to Mrs Cursiter and yourself

Yours sincerely
Robert Rendall

Kirkwall, 7 September 1963

Dear Dr Cursiter,

For a week or more you have been very much in my mind—not with anything in view, but simply in friendly thought. You know how these unprompted impulses come.

Since I returned from Italy what I saw of Michaelangelo's work has haunted my mind, especially those large massive sculptures in the Academia at Florence—and in the various churches & chapels there. To fall under the spell of those noble figures struggling to emerge from the imprisoning rock was an experience—as also it was to have a close-up of the very chisel-marks and tooling of the great master. One felt how much his inspiration and craftsmanship went together. How difficult to attain this balance between the two!

Have you read Irvine Stone's "I, Michaelangelo, Sculptor"—the sequel to "The Agony and Ecstasy"—in which is presented a chronological series of Michaelangelo's letters? They document (and illustrate in a remarkable way) the story told in "The Agony and Ecstasy", and make delightful reading. They take one right into Michaelangelo's private life—and into his very habits of thought. The book is now in the County library—but still in my hands here at Dawnvale! It contains, too, a fine selection of his sonnets in what I take to be a new translation—very fresh, direct, & modern. The translations by J. A. Symonds & even by Wordsworth are much more artificial . . .

My own private muse has been playing a game with me—sometimes peeping provocatively round the corner, and then dashing away out of sight . . .

Kirkwall, 5 March 1965

Dear Dr Cursiter,

The 'excitement' of using a brush has again taken a firm grip of my imagination and at long last I am finding some leisure to attempt some practice painting . . .

All being well I hope to have two good spells in Westray and to spend some whole days over at the west crags and also along at Aikerness in the north.

The brown trout season opens in a week's time and I look forward to many of those dreamy idle days on the loch which are one of Orkney's charming experiences. Since I retired I have not spent a full summer in the islands—ten weeks in Italy last year and seven the year before. But this one I do not even intend to go south but to sink myself into our beloved Orkney. Even in winter . . . . . . !!! for last Sunday I got stuck in a snow-drift on the Lyde road—we had to abandon the car and face a blinding blizzard on foot: eventually we reached a farm where perforce I had to stay marooned overnight—quite an adventure . . .

Ward 5, Eastbank Hospital, Kirkwall.
[1965]

Dear Dr Cursiter,

I recognized the handwriting at once—and opened with pleasure your kind letter of farewell: the 'pleasure' was in the letter, not the farewell! I, too, have felt much as you have done the frustration of hopes for the summer—my first whole summer in Orkney for three years, and which I intended devoting to trout-fishing on the lochs and painting on our shores.

I'm glad to hear how the chapel project[1] is getting on and feel sure that it will add something permanent (and fitting) to our Cathedral interior. I sense your great love of *designing* your projected works and the pleasure it gives you. It makes me think of similar preoccupation in the old masters like Cellini whose genius branched out into so many forms of art.

Saturday will complete my fourth week here and it looks as if I shall be here for two or three weeks yet. The treatment I am receiving is very gradually proving helpful and I am quite happy

& contented here—and receiving every attention. Mr Konstam[2] was up one day with four books in German and these have diverted my idle hours—especially one on German Prose (The Oxford Book of) which has interesting extracts from a wide range of German writers from Luther to Rilke.

When I get home I shall have to take things easy for a bit, owing to heart condition but I look forward to doing some more writing on Orkney. In my early days I wandered round most of our shoreline and along most of our moorland ridges— memories of those idyllic days still remain with me and I should like to share them with others. At that time my interest in antiquities was stronger than it is now (from an *active* point of view). It was then that I discovered the Wideford Hill flint field and then I opened the broch of Gurness. All this will leave scope to record the deeds (and misdeeds) of the OAS.

I have a young friend—now in the Board of Agriculture office—who is following the pattern of my own early days and wandering far and near over our hilltops—exploring and finding new aspects of our island geography. Most Orkney people now confine their goings to places which a motor-car can take them to and there are great stretches of moorland and clifftop which are more or less *terra incognita* to Orcadians themselves.

But enough—I am allowing myself to wander away in words! Hoping that Mrs Cursiter and yourself will have a pleasant winter in the south.

Yours sincerely
Robert Rendall

An epigram in A Book of Persian Verse tempted me to write an Orkney Variant

> On meädow-girse and fields o' bere
> The rip'nan sun shines doun alike,
> And nourishes wi' equal care
> Wild floo'ers apae this aald hill dyke.

Only—the Persian one had roses and the desert thistle!

R.R.

---

[1] Stanley Cursiter was designing the woodcarvings of three figures for St Rognvald's Chapel in St Magnus Cathedral.

[2] The resident surgeon in Orkney.

TO HIS FAMILY

Robert Rendall wrote a large number of letters to various members of his family when away from them, and two letters from this correspondence have been selected. The first letter, telling of some comments made on his early poetry by the editor of the popular religious magazine **Great Thoughts,** *is to his mother and his brother and was written when he was on HMS* **Imperieuse** *during World War I. The second letter is an open letter to his family describing his experiences during his first visit to England and Germany in 1930. During his journey he stayed with relatives in London and at the Christian Brethren Bible School at Wiedenest in Germany.*

HMS Imperieuse
c/o G.P.O.
5 March, 1918

Dear Mother & Willie,

I received your welcome letters last night and I had one from Mr Wm Mainland[1] also. I was glad to know of your good meetings on Sunday and surprised to hear of Willie's closing the Sunday School. You have evidently been doing quite a lot of visiting.

Bridger and I had a nice talk together last night. He is a very fine fellow. Alec spoke at our meeting last Sunday on the text 'Seek ye the Lord while He may be found' and did very well.

And mother, I have something which I think will interest you, but you, Willie, may find no interest in it whatever. Now, had you read Great Thoughts properly, there would have been no need for me to tell you. But since you have not mentioned it in any letter, I presume you never came across it. Have I raised your curiosity? Well. Let me tell you all about it.

Some time ago, after much weighing up of pros and cons, I decided to send some of my verses to the Editor of Great Thoughts for criticism. Ah. Now you know why I have been looking for that paper every week. Patience has its reward and his judgment upon it far exceeded my expectations. I sent three pieces, two being lyrics and one a sonnet. He points out two minor errors in the first two which he says an unreflecting reader might pass over, but finds no fault with the sonnet.

Perhaps the best plan is to let you know his own words. Of the first lyric he says 'You rhyme in a dainty fashion and the lyric as a whole creates quite a good impression.' Then he continues 'Your Shakespearean sonnet, written on the prospect of distant hills, is quite good; indeed, it comes near to being excellent. It is conceived in a highly poetic and reverent mood and is expressed with taste and judgment.'

Naturally, it has encouraged me very much and shown me the small blemishes which I am apt to make. I thought I would keep it a secret from you until I knew the result. Now, Willie, I can fancy I hear you saying how glad you are that you will not be in the house when I get my leave or you would be pestered with my verses.

Of course I cannot think of anything else to write about tonight so I will close in highest exuberance with best love

from your affectionate
old Robert.

---

[1] A member of the Kirkwall Brethren.

[1930]

27th May '30: Left Kirkwall Pier 6.00 a.m. by S.S. St Rognvald . . . We reached Aberdeen about 5.40 . . . and boarded the 7.50 train for Euston. A commercial gentleman from London and myself were the only occupants of our carriage, and we both secured an extra pillow and blanket, and tipped the attendant to bring us a cup of tea in the morning . . .

28th May: . . . Was wakened at 7 a.m. by "Cup of Tea, sir!" Yawned, dressed myself, sat up, and took notice of the world. "Now," said I, "For my first sight of old England," and up sprang the blind. Immediately there leapt to my mind the lines of Quiller Couch's, "O heart of pastoral England", for just at that moment we were passing through a lovely stretch of green meadowlands, sprinkled here and there with groups of dreamy looking trees. White-blossomed may-trees leaned out over the fields, from the midst of closely-clipped green English hedges; a fold of drowsy sheep was succeeded by a pasture of kine, the young calves standing stock still among the short green grass: farm-houses with steeply-ridged roofs and thick square chimney-tops flew past the carriage windows, then walls of weathered red brick contrasting pleasingly with the verdure of the fields. And what was that? A fairy-ring under the trees—I almost expected to glimpse Oberon, king of the fairies next. After this I saw Bridges' "Clear and gentle stream", or at least one like it. This enchanted land held me in spell for quite a while, and I now understand for the first time in my life how such fine poetry as that of our English poets has come to be written. The inspiration is here. But the train flies on, London draws nearer, and I must have a wash . . .

My general impressions of London are too vague yet to put into words. But I will focus my mind on this amazing city before I leave it. The streams of traffic hold one's attention—they flow on for ever, and not as in Glasgow with periodic hold-ups. The force may be intermittent, but the stream itself flows steadily on. Aeroplanes hum overhead—no one heeds them; gay buses rattle on—one merely dodges them. The streets swarm with message-boys; the lanes pour out lorry after lorry, piled high with bales and boxes; the pavements are black with business and professional men. Glasgow is not to be mentioned when London is under notice . . .

31st May: I have had a good night's sleep, and feel in good form for my journey. We arrive Dover 12.11 p.m., leave 12.30, arrive Ostend 4.5 and then straight to Deutschland . . .

I have been greatly taken with the German people & their manner of life. They have many little customs of courtesy which we entirely lack, & I am beginning to pick these up. In fact, the best part of my holiday has been my intercourse with the people (not that I haven't thoroughly enjoyed the sights—far from that!), & in noticing their manner of life. The German people live very much more naturally than we, & are not so troubled with self-consciousness. You don't meet the superior English gentleman, staring at you with unwinking eye over the Times, *here*—No, everyone is friendly & a German railway journey is a treat—everyone is more or less animated. For instance, in our carriage to Wiedenest this afternoon we had a company of 'wanderers'. Holidays here are spent in 'Wandering' with Rucksack from place to place. I've met dozens upon dozens of such groups of 'young folk' carrying banners & guitars. But I digress. A 3rd Class carriage here has rough wooden seats & *no* partition, 30 or so in each wagon. A scramble for window & corner seats & we're off. Young bronze faced men with *nothing* but short shorts, a vivid blue or green

open-necked shirt & a pair of sandals— young women with BIG
Rucksacks, & dressed in coloured linen frocks with tight-high-
waisted bodices, & gay striped full skirts—the peasant type.
Rucksacks are deposited in racks and under seats—swigs are
taken at water-bottles & we settle down to the journey. The
guitar is thrummed & everyone breaks out into old German
folk-songs. My word, it was great, with the fine deep bass voices
& clear trebles going strong. They sang lustily & naturally.
Then we had a solo full of pathos, sung by a fair-haired Saxon
with blue eyes & leather trousers! ha ha! It was simply great . . .

I missed Ronald[1] very much after we parted company, we
had such a good time together. I must say he looked after me
well!!! & kept me from the temptations of booksellers etc. Alas!
Alas! But I'm in Wiedenest now where no bookshops are.

I'll have lots of news to tell you of the Christians here. The
Russian refugees have some terrible tales to tell. The newspaper
reports are not one little bit exaggerated in telling of the actual
'torture' of our Russian brethren. They have been forced by
torture (some of them) to dig their own graves in the ice, strip,
lie down in them and die frozen, & have been so exhausted that
they could not resist. So pray on for Russia . . .

Sunday. This has been another good day & I have had
walks & conversations with Germans, Hungarians, Russians,
Mennonites, & so forth, & have gathered a lot of interesting &
out of the way information with regard to the conditions of life
in Eastern Europe. Several of the Russians here have had
dramatic escapes. One cannot ask them to relate their
adventures, but I have collected lots of incidents from odd table
conversation. All the languages are going at mealtime &
the cross table talk, explanations & interpretations of difficult
words is simply great. The people here on the continent are
great linguists. We should be ashamed of ourselves—our
insularity in respect of modern languages is a byword, and put
down to fancied superiority!!! . . .

But most of all have I been impressed by the courtesy of
the people, that is, by the many little actions of deference they
preserve in the ordinary ways of life. When being introduced to
a man one bows slightly before shaking hands, & then again
when shaking hands. Entering a room is almost a ceremony.
"Bitte"—Please—Please very much—If you hand the bread to
anyone at table, or confer a favour, you must make it appear as
if you were receiving a favour & say "Bitte Schön" please very

much. Meals are never served in one's plate but ALWAYS in a dish—a good custom, for then one can eat as little (or as much!) as one pleases, without embarrassment . . .

Here in Wiedenest they have the old custom of a very short grace (1 or 2 sentences) before meals & after meals a short prayer, 4 or 5 verses of scripture, & a hymn.

The young fellows here know all about our poets & are interested in the cultures of *other* nations than their own. One Hungarian here, by name Vitezlsia Lajos, speaks *fluently* in German, Hungarian, Latin (I heard a Latin conversation last night), Greek, Hebrew, *Old* English, English, & *Old* German. He also has a good nodding acquaintance with Spanish, Hieroglyphic (Egyptian), Arabic, French & Italian. This is not a joke, but solemn fact! I may say I've also had interesting talks with Belgians, etc. I can count at least 13 different nationalities within a 100 yards of where I am sitting, & I can assure you my little German has been very useful to me . . .

The local papers came today & I was interested to hear of the success of the excavations at Aikerness. I was in a museum in Köln on Thursday last week—my *first* Museum in Germany—it was a flint one & they had an excellent collection. The curator & venerable old gent with a white beard was particularly kind, could speak no English, but opened cases for me (quite on his own) and in every way tried to show me the collection. I was able to make myself understood to him in German, & he took me to special cases for pygmy flints etc, & I've found some of the types I have, especially the interesting small knife with the handle. Then I also saw flaked *clear* rock crystal—just like the piece I found.

But I must go off to bed!

---

[1] Ronald Mooney, son of John Mooney, later a research chemist with ICI.

Wiedenest

TO SIR JAMES FERGUSSON

After the Second World War, Sir James Fergusson (1904-73) was a leader-writer with **The Glasgow Herald** *and also had responsibility for the poetry in the newspaper's supplement. He was appointed Keeper of the Records of Scotland in 1949 and he succeeded to the baronetcy of Kilkerran, Ayrshire in 1951. He edited an anthology of Scottish poetry,* **The Green Garden** *(1946), and wrote a number of elegant historical essays. After Robert Rendall sent a copy of* **Country Sonnets** *to him, the two men corresponded intensively and at length over a period of several months. Rendall turned to Fergusson for advice on his future direction as a poet while Fegusson gave Rendall strong encouragement to continue writing. They remained friends throughout Rendall's lifetime and continued to correspond regularly.*

[*Kirkwall, April 1947*]

Dear Mr Fergusson,

I have just received a letter from our mutual friend Mr Stanley Cursiter, who informs me that he has written you on my behalf regarding my recently-published "Country Sonnets". I had desired to get some honestly-expressed informed criticism of the poems, and also advice how best to introduce the book to circles outside our islands, should it be thought to merit wider circulation. [Although I followed with interest] your contribution to the "Plastic Scots" correspondence in The Glasgow Herald earlier in the year, I had not cared to write you without introduction. As advised by Mr Cursiter I send you herewith a copy of my book—duly autographed in case you care to have it for your library.

The first edition of just over 500 copies sold out from the publishers within a week or two, so I am having a second impression made (also of 500 copies) which will be ready some time about the end of May. This will be uniform with the first impression except for the correction of a misplaced line in "Summer Flowers". The favourable reception given the book by fellow Orcadians, and the consequent rapid local sale, hindered me from sending it for review to publications outside the islands, but now I feel that I should like to send it for this purpose to some Scottish literary journals. I still hold a few

81

copies: these might well be so used. If some were sent for review *now*, and the reviews proved favourable I might have extracts from these used on the back of the jacket for the second impression. This might help sales. One of the local booksellers still has a few copies left which would meet any immediate enquiries raised by such reviews, and a second impression will be out, I hope, by May. I should therefore be extremely grateful if you could suggest where best the book might be 'placed' for review.

Also, the book being published locally, I am uncertain of the correct procedure for getting it taken up by booksellers in, say, Edinburgh and Glasgow. Could you advise me regarding this?

Except for "The Fisherman" I have not attempted anything in our local dialect, but the Plastic Scots controversy has wakened a fresh interest in the possibilities of the Orkney Norn. We have, as you will know, a vocabulary (still in use) of words and phrases purely Norse in origin—as well as typical Scots words. We also have certain inflections and grammatical constructions native to the islands. But while we use these unconsciously in everyday speech it is difficult to recall them when they are wanted in poetic composition. Do you not think that where the living language is "mixed" all the elements should find place in the poetic vocabulary? To me this seems the true plasticism? Old native forms can well be used if they still contain a nuance of meaning or feeling otherwise inexpressible, but surely not to the exclusion of enrichment from other sources, even if one of these should be common English. This is not to say that I do not admire the effects gained from the use of old Scots words with their rugged couthiness and homeliness of feeling. But just to use them for the sake of antique effect or because of political feeling seems retrogressive. We in Orkney might then refuse to write in verse except in the pure Norn. Or should we? In case it may interest you I shall send you with this a recent poem in the living tongue,[1] but just for your private eye as I have promised it to my friend, Mr Ernest Marwick, who hopes soon to publish an Anthology of Orkney Poetry from early times on.

Is it too much to hope that you may favour me with a personal criticism of "Country Sonnets" both from the viewpoint of its imaginative content and of its prosody? This would render me a great service for possible future work, since, though I submit my compositions to as drastic self-criticism as I can, it is difficult to get outside of one's own mind. A fresh approach is usually illuminating, and the more so when it is based on a wider experience.

I trust that these few personal requests will not intrude too much on your time.

Yours sincerely,
Robert Rendall

[1] 'Cragsman's Widow'. The earlier lack of mention of this poem (in this, a draft copy of the letter) is probably explained by the promise to let Ernest Marwick publish it first. See letter to Ernest Marwick dated June 1947.

Kirkwall, 23 April 1947

Dear Mr Fergusson,

Your letter of the 21st., received today, ties together all the loose ends . . .

Now about your queries! Bridges' influence on my work has, I suspect, been indirect, lying rather in the example of meticulous craftsmanship, though I have admired some of his later metrical experiments in "New Verse Written in 1921" and in "October", but I have never been *quite* able to follow the formal technique by which he gains his effects, which appeal very strongly to me. My own "Country Burial" was an attempt in that direction, and "Beauty's Quest" is somewhat Bridgesque, isn't it? Walter de la Mare I like very much. Yes, Blunden is a favourite. I never weary of Masefield. Day Lewis' "Translation of the Georgics" to me reads well, but it may be because it is the "Georgics"! "The Greek Anthology", in translation, had a direct influence on me in my twenties in showing the virtues of "tightness". But, as you have probably seen for yourself, I have not consciously imitated any particular poet, but followed my own bent and sought to train my ear by listening to the music, catching what to me seemed best in any of them . . .

Kirkwall, 25 April 1947

Dear Mr Fergusson,

Our letters have now crossed more than once, but I think that despite our somewhat bewildering wealth of topics we both know where we are! . . .

I got your telegram yesterday, and shall await your letter before I post this. But in the meantime I must reply to some points raised in your interesting letter of the 23rd. To return to "Bridges". No, I have not read through the "Testament of Beauty", but only bits of it, and that a good while ago. But I have long promised myself that pleasure. But the poems of Bridges that have intrigued me are those mentioned in my last letter, to which "Cheddar Pinks" could be added as it is in the same metrical type. I have admired these immensely, but been baffled by their technique. I can read them to myself with the greatest delight; there is a freedom of rhythm which admits of variety and so avoids a set jog-trot movement, and yet—seemingly—a very strict rule the neglect of which immediately offends the ear. Am I right in thinking that this type of prosody rises out of his study of the prosody of Milton, the exposition of which in this "Miltonic Prosody" is painfully difficult to read but intensely fascinating? It has been my hope for years—unsatisfied so far—that I shall yet get more than a glimmering of what he is at. Your reference to his 12-syllabled blank verse makes me hope that you may sometime, when sufficiently at leisure, send me some technical comments on it. As you remark, it takes an expert to handle it, and while I have wit enough to see that I cannot hope to equal Bridges' use of it, I feel that here is a noble instrument that could be put to good use.

I hope to listen in to the broadcast next Tuesday evening,[1] although with my deafness I find listening in extremely difficult. I'm glad that Douglas Young sends you an occasional poem. It's a pity when a group become so self-centred that they cannot appreciate other forms of art than their own. The *relations* of truth are so much more important than its distinctions, however important these also may be. The Plastic Scots group might have found more general acceptance if they had made their experiments an enrichment of an already existing tradition. I like Lewis Spence's poem in last week's "Herald", as "faerie" stuff needs to be really well done if it is to rise above mere sentimentality, and this sustains the central image with evocative words and phrases.

Thank you for making clear what you meant by "enlargement of poetic vocabulary"; I concur with your remarks thereupon, and value the suggestion. Bridges' device when using simple language seems to have been the introduction of words indicating 'colour' e.g. "the red rust of the iron wreck"; "the whitened planking of the mill"; "flame-throated robin"; "Spring goeth all in white". These leap to my mind. His five books of "Shorter Poems" are full of this, and the indirect way also in which he 'suggests' colour is notable. In my "Orkney after the War"[2] you may not find your rose-beds, but there are at least a few dandelions!

I must say how much I appreciated in your first letter the reference to my "Sonnets on Christian Faith".[3] It has been my regret for years that I have not been able to write a direct poem on Christian feeling and conviction anything approaching those written on other themes, and all the more so since to me such feeling and conviction have been the salt of life. I contribute occasionally expository articles to religious magazines, and find my greatest delight in studying "the Book". It is good to meet one who holds similar sentiments.

It may interest you to know which poems in my book have caught the public imagination *here*. Setting aside individual favourites of several friends, Varro, Siberian Spring, Winter, Night-wind, Orkney, and Country Burial, there have been two which seem to have captured everyone—Birsay, and The Fisherman. The former evidently expressed for many what you term "inarticulate" thoughts, and though I took a slight coolness toward it myself because of its quick popularity I find myself coming back to it again. Birsay, as you may know, is *the* place in Orkney where there is a genuine sense of escape from the sophistications of modern life, so that the popularity of the poem may be due partly to its evocative effect on those that know Birsay . . .

---

[1] 'Arts Review', in which Fergusson reviewed *Country Sonnets*. In fact the review was delayed until 21 May.

[2] The reference is unclear—possibly an unpublished poem which Rendall had sent to Fergusson.

[3] 'Sonnets on the Christian Faith' was the title of a group of poems in *Country Sonnets*.

[Kirkwall, May, 1947]

Dear Mr Fergusson,

Now that the second impression of "Country Sonnets" has been launched upon an innocent and unsuspecting public, I feel that I owe you some account of my reactions to the whole event, and in particular to the part you have so kindly filled in reviewing the book. I read with extreme pleasure but with a curious sense of detachment your delightful and sensitively worded review in the Thursday page of the "Herald". You certainly have an uncanny insight into the working methods of a poet's mind, and express in words many of the unspoken ideas that, some consciously and some unconsciously, have influenced my writing. Your references to Orkney have struck a most responsive chord up here, and we rejoice to think that, while remaining a Scotsman, you recognise the unique characteristics of our island life, even as we, while cherishing our distinctive local tradition, remember that we, too, share with you in a larger heritage.

I gravely doubt whether my powers will prove sufficient to produce another such volume until some considerable time has passed, but I should be ungrateful to those who have offered me such kind encouragement were I not to have the task seriously in mind, and you may be assured that, as I have leisure for devoting myself to it, I shall pursue it eagerly. Only, in the future as in the past, I shall pursue my own bent as honestly as I can, as only by so doing can one avoid forced and artificial work. Yet I have been very much helped by your assessment of particular poems, and have found fresh 'direction' from some of your comments that may enable me to explore fresh ground. The solitary poet is too apt, especially in sonnets, to give purely personal impressions of life and nature which may, or may not, also reflect a more universal note, but too much of this is apt to become egotistic in feeling. It was because of this that I adopted the "imaginative soliloquy" approach seen in "Varro" and "St Gregory". While drawn from classical sources, they had immediate situations in view, but each being transposed to an objective person, avoided the personal reference.

I have already written you about some of my views on dialect verse, but would like to form a 'canon' for myself before venturing too far in that field. Among the old Norse words that survive in our local speech is a large group describing the moods and sounds and movements of the sea, another relating to weather conditions, and still another picturesque group hitting off piquantly the manifold vagaries of human behaviour. These have great descriptive powers, and are very evocative, but their use is only justified, I think, by making them express some definite imaginative idea or situation. If this is forgotten they can become a positive temptation by reason of their very picturesqueness.

This summer I shall not have the leisure to devote to 'country living' that I have had during the past few years. I live alone with my mother, who is now over 80 years of age, and as she now needs to stay in the town and requires constant attention, it does not seem likely that I shall get the conditions which—to me—are a pre-requisite for the *writing* of verse. But I am keeping a detailed record of possible subjects and of ideas and experiences that demand poetic expression. These can well lie dormant in the mind, and one day, unexpectedly, when out in the country, up they will come and the old torment return! Generally the whole framework of the poem will suggest itself then, rapidly (and even the rhyme structure be seen in its general entirety), though with gaps; as if the whole thing had been worked out in some secret cave! If this 'moment' is grasped, and recorded before the excitement goes, then there is a nucleus to work from, and the real task begins which I find most laborious and which enslaves me until I get it fully accomplished. "St Gregory" came up like a djinn out of the bottle (figuratively, of course!) one morning on awakening from sleep, and fortunately I had sufficient sense not to continue in a half-dream but to stretch out for an old envelope at my bedside and feverishly get down the structure of it. The whole rhyme pattern of the octave presented itself just as it appears, but I afterwards found the sestet most intractable to get into its proper shape.

I have long felt that I would like to master some pedestrian metre that could be used on occasion for longer pieces of verse that did not demand so concentrated expression as the sonnet or short lyric. Even Horace—in his epodes, wasn't it? professed to use such a metre. It would be exceedingly useful for certain classes of subject, of which I have a few in mind. Masefield has it. Robert Frost, too, has a narrative style of his own. Bridges, more difficultly, uses his quantitative measures for this purpose.

But it is fatally easy to descend into a jingle, and to lose the rapidity so essential if—as Q so constantly reminds us—we are to avoid "the capital difficulty of verse" . . .

THE LOWER P'LACE, BIRSAY c.1915

TO ERNEST AND JANETTE MARWICK

Ernest Marwick (1915-77), scholar, journalist and broadcaster, studied the social history and folklore of Orkney and was the author of 'Journey from Serfdom' (1954), a study of Orkney in the nineteenth century, and **Orkney and Shetland Folklore** *(1975), the work that he is chiefly remembered for. Marwick was largely self-educated, having worked first as a farmer and then as a bookshop assistant; he studied at Newbattle Abbey, however, during 1953-4 while Edwin Muir was Warden. In the early 1960s Marwick left* **The Orkney Herald** *(where he had been working) to do freelance writing and lecturing in, among other places, Norway and Aberdeen. It was while working on his first book,* **An Anthology of Orkney Verse** *(1949), that he became close friends with Robert Rendall. In 1943 Marwick had married Janette Sandison (1898-1981). Their house was near Rendall's and he was in daily contact with them. Marwick and Rendall shared an interest in literature, religion, painting, photography, and Orkney life and culture.*

Kirkwall [June, 1947]

Dear Ernest,

You must be feeling like a "hermit" in your little cell, but I hope that very soon you may be able to renounce your vows of solitude and restore yourself to your friends. With the better weather you should make a more rapid recovery.

Last night I was busy on my not ancestral but bachelor acres & got a whole field sown. This year I have been kept from the farm but my love of the life, I find, is undiminished.

While I look to seeing you do some first-class original verse once you have got your anthology launched upon an unsuspecting public! I hope you will put the Muse into a dark hole until you have recovered health. Although pleasurable, writing verse is a tax on physical strength—or so I find it—and from a life-long experience of minor illnesses or at any rate not over robust health I have learned the wisdom of completely relaxing literary interests at certain times. Not that I always act upon that wisdom, Ernest!

Thank you for your consent to the publication of "Cliff Accident".[1] Mr Fergusson wrote several times before I took definite action in the matter. He has suggested some textual emendations in "spelling" and made some very illuminating observations on the relation of dialect poems to national literature . . .

Mother attains her 80th birthday on Saturday: I hope to celebrate it with her up at Miss Cooper's in Birsay.

Kind thoughts

Robert

---

[1] The poem was published in *The Glasgow Herald* with the title 'Cragsman's Widow'.

DAWNVALE
KIRKWALL

[*Kirkwall, c1948*]

. . . the features of the rainbow cliff in all their native
beauty are now gradually emerging to the astonished gaze of an
admiring public.¹ And in view of the unwonted expenditure of
energy, nervous and physical—art, they say, is exhausting—I am
repleting my prostrate system with a switched egg and some
warm milk, the which I am consuming as I type this. Night
draws on apace and I have yet to record a syllabic effusion in
verse before I betake myself to the land of Dream, so I must
pop (which reminds me I got a belated delivery of still another
book on Dialect and Language; I must have applied for quite a
number at various times!) my brushes into a PERMANENT
jam-jar of turps to save daily cleaning . . .

When I think on the Alps that HAVEN'T been painted,
and the still inarticulate experiences awaiting poetic expression, I
am surprised that the Labour Government doesn't acquire a
better sense of proportion and instead of recommending higher
standards of living, (which only means still higher peaks behind)
advise the folk to aim at simpler living (what they are actually
doing, of course) so as to have time for what is called—by those
who do it!— CREATIVE WORK. After all, Ernest, what is an
extra kipper for breakfast against a new poem? Alas, I must
down to the shop again—and the money-making, as old
Masefield puts it . . .

I don't suppose you ever realised that you are that
mysterious thing which good people sometimes call "an answer
to prayer". Ever since I lost James Tulloch, the friend of my
youth, I have never had an intimate 'personal' friend and the
middle part of my life was very much of a blank as regards all
those interests that we have in common and also, as you may
guess, for an outlet to my natural nonsense and hair-brained
tendencies . . . The other day I suddenly realised that YOU
were the veritable answer combining as you do that spice of
'wickedness'! with genuine zeal for those things that make life
worth while; and also that I had not only gained a brother, but,
as is usual in matters of this kind ("more than ye can ask or
think") a sister as well—something much needed to complete
my education, for sisters are proverbially and commendably
outspoken in keeping their brothers in proper order, both with
the world and with themselves . . .

By the way, I have a book now that would greatly interest

you: a birdwatching one by Eric Hosking and C. Newberry. Excellent reading. What do you think of the migration of birds as a metaphor for the soul's flight through time, or, if you are impatient with metaphysics, as a symbol of the Orkney way of life. The scattering out into the world and later on the return of the exiles. ? ? ?

But it is time to stop, so goodnight,

Robert

[1] Rendall was referring to a painting he was working on.

Leytonstone
London
[c1953]

Dear Janette,

Its about time I was coming back to Orkney for I have been feeling full of beans and mischief, having greatly enjoyed my time so far. Down here in London the time has been most leisurely for there is little to do and little to see, which makes one take things easy, and just sit about mooning away the time. On Tuesday Mr Watson and I spent the whole day in Kew Gardens, having lunch and tea in the open air. A most delightful outing, with the trees in their Spring green and many covered with blossom. The only place that I have seen that I would dare to set alongside Birsay.

Then yesterday, following my rule of only One thing a day, we called at the House of Commons and after the usual leisurely preliminaries were conducted duly to the Foreign Diplomats Gallery (the House of Commons is becoming intelligent these days, and realising the uniqueness of Orkney!), where we had an excellent view of the chamber, and observed the cut and thrust of debate regulated by the chair, which was treated with marked respect. But there was great freedom with occasional dramatic touches . . .

My shell ploys are going well and I am about to set off for South Kensington[1] to keep an appointment there. In Liverpool I got a lot of work done. Spent six solid hours one day looking

91

over shells, with only a hasty thermos tea for mid-day meal; and part of another day.

I hope to have a day in Edinburgh on my way north, and to see George Brown at Newbattle Abbey, and also to have a look at the Scottish Exhibition of paintings. Stanley Cursiter has three in it, two portraits, one of an interior of the Cathedral, and, bless you, sensible man, one of Skipi Geo . . .

[1] The Natural History Museum, South Kensington

Kirkwall, 30 December 1953

My dear Ernest, and elusive Christmas wanderer!

I am sending this to Glasgow in the hope that it will reach you there. Before I leave for the wilds (tomorrow) I must give you an account of how the Christmas season has gone here. For myself, I heaved a big sigh of relief when it was all over. More and more I come to think of an ideal Xmas as being one spent at a cheerie fireside among a few intimates and no arduous social duties or obligations. This must be a merchant's dream of Christmas . . .

Last night I had an almost unexpected visitation of the Muse which filled me with the intensest excitement I have felt for years and for a few minutes made me quite fey, the real furore poeticus, if that be the proper gender, O worthy Latinist! I felt a physical dilation of the heart over it and was quite intoxicated with the suddenness of the attack. NO, it wasn't the turkey, though Embla[1] suggested that, NOR was it home brew. I almost gave up the idea of tea till the deed was done, but squashed it until I had taken some nourishment, then down the typewriter, and almost straightforward, with only a slight alteration in one line, wrote the enclosed sonnet.[2] I had intended a stanzaic lyric, but the sonnet came out practically readymade. I never saw it happening quite like that before. The evening was to have been devoted to sober shell work but was *ruined*.

Immediately I DASHED up to George[3] to get the thing off my chest which was much constricted by it (although I had already visited him during the afternoon), but when I got there I was so completely out of breath that I was physically EXHAUSTED and could only lie and pant for a while to George's amazement, for he did not know what on earth was the matter at that late hour. You see, I missed the cooling influence of Westermill and Janette's bland voice innocently enquiring, "Cup of tea?" George must have been highly amused. Then I had to call on Embla and inflict it on her, to her great amusement, and finally on poor Bessie:[4] then I partially subsided like a floundered fish.

Of course this does not necessarily mean that the poem is absolutely IT; it was the excitement that accompanied the writing of it. I think that it was George who told me that you had been writing some poems yourself: you'll be sending us some specimens, won't you?

It is almost poet time.

RR

---

[1] Embla Mooney, daughter of John Mooney.
[2] The text of 'Renewal' was typed immediately beneath the signature to this letter.
[3] George Mackay Brown was in hospital in Kirkwall. He gave an account of this incident in *An Orkney Tapestry* (1969), pp 168-9.
[4] Bessie Costie, a near neighbour of Rendall and the Marwicks. Her sister, Christina, wrote prose and poetry in dialect.

Birsay
[c1955]

My dear Ernest,

It seems fantanstic to write you when we shall again be seeing one another so soon, but these last two or three days I have been missing your company, and wondering how you are getting on. I have greatly enjoyed my time up here. George would have told you that I called along his home when in Stromness last Friday with the Coupers. We had taken an afternoon run down to see their sisters at Citadel after the death of their cousin in Marwick. I just idled about the street, did a few messages, bought a copy of Stewart of Baldynneis for 6d at Jim Stevenson's old shop, and two cloak and dagger tales (Nelson Series) from Rae's, secondhand at 9d. The Museum was closed up as they have lost their caretaker. I had a look in to J.G.M.,[1] whom I found cheerful and brisk as ever. An old man of 97 walked in—a Mr Matches—and began to talk about Skatehorn.[2]

My time has been well filled. The recent gales have made beachcombing arduous but profitable and kept me occupied during the early forenoons. There is certainly a fascination about the ploy. Trout fishing finished last week and the weather has been too rough for much fishing from the rocks, but yesterday afternoon all the conditions were extra favourable, low spring tide (enabling me to get to Longaber, which is usually inaccessible). Weather was calm, low tide co-incided with late evening, the wind was in the right direction, the sea moderate. So I fished deep with bait and got 26 big cuithes including some dundies.[3] The cubbie was full to overflowing as they were BIG fish. The other night I saw a lunar rainbow which is always a pretty sight. Have you seen one? Then this week I have really WORKED HARD at my shell book, and got a good part of the final MS done for Prof. Edwards. The work in connection with it is a good deal complicated, involving much checking up of details, but I see the end of the long tunnel.

Between times I have been doing some cleaning up in Miss Couper's garden and some wood-chopping. When splitting some big logs I have secured the valves and pallets of certain Teredo worms, which are a genus of shell-fish. The other day Harvey's cat took in a small bird, but no one seemed to know what kind it was. So I sent it off to J.G.M. with a note and we shall see if it is, as it may be, a ridiculously common species or if it is some sort of migrant: I am totally ignorant of the birds.

I had a nice letter the other day from my friends at Pesaro, and also a letter from Algeria. Last Sunday I was up at the kirk abune the hill. During the afternoon I visited the Hunters of Flaws and in the evening read the Schersing of Trew Felicitie by John Stewart of Baldynneis: it is a sort of early Pilgrim's Progress with a touch of Spenser in it. The day before yesterday I had the boat taken home from the loch and it now is laid up in a nook behind the sea-wall in one of Mrs Comloquoy's yards. It will be near at hand for overhaul and painting. During the earlier part of my holiday I got the spoots,[4] door etc of my house painted. This completed exterior painting of the house which now looks neat to the eye.

All being well I hope to see you on Sunday afternoon and to get all your news and my usual teasing from Janette: I hope that she is completely well again. Oh, by the way, I got a big legal-looking document the other day, two of them, AUTHOR-

PUBLISHER contract, 6d stamp and all that. The terms are quite generous.

Looking forward to seeing you all again,

Robert

[1] James George Marwick (1876-1960), provost of Stromness and writer of a weekly nature column in *The Orcadian*.

[2] A well-known tramp of bygone days.

[3] 'Cuithes' and 'dundies' are Orkney names for various stages in the development of coalfish (*Pollachius virens*).

[4] *spoots* (Orkney dialect): gutters and drainpipes.

Kirkwall, 27 August 1955

My dear Ernest and Janette,

You certainly have caught the weather in a good mood, and not, as she so often is in the West Highlands, in a scowling mood. Today's post brought three items, one from yourselves, one from the Sheriff at Tenerife (Spanish spelling) and one from, who do you think, A.D.[1] of the Glasgow Herald saying my pen has been too idle! Alas for their hope of a poem in my present bogged mental state. I may send them something in prose if only I could find the time.

My only time in the West was a fortnight in Wester Ross, which has the same beauty of scenery and the same Free Presbyterianism as you appear to have met with, rigid views but very kindly people. I can well understand your frequent runs over to Skye, and how you are baffled by the splendour of its mountains. Probably you would find in time, once the original glamour had worn off that you preferred the more subtle beauty of our Orkney landscape and its permanent austerities: at least I do so, even after having seen some magnificent scenery in one place or another.

Plockton looks lovely—except that the horizon is blocked by mountains! But that may be due to the angle of vision in the postcard . . .

[1] Anne Donaldson

Kirkwall, 14 June 1961

My dear Ernest,

It's wearing on for 1 o'clock (Wednesday) but I simply must send you a wee line to say how pleased I am to hear that you are again improving in health. This forenoon I was a wee look along Westermill and as usual dear Janette was presiding over the TEAPOT and having a refresher, so R.R. had a cup, too, about hands, as they say.

Somehow, with visitors of one sort and another I seem to be kept in continual motion and have not had many Wasdale retreats. A missionary friend from Tanganyika is in Orkney at the moment, so I have been acting as a sort of pilot for his meetings. He is a very fine fellow with a disarming guilessness (how's that for a neologism?) of manner that makes it very pleasant to be in his company . . .

I have ordered my microscope—a stunner, I feel sure, and also a high intensity low voltage lamp for use in the dark nights of winter when my famous study will also incorporate a scientific laboratory. So between paintings and drawings on the wall, poetry and theology in the shelves, shells and seaweeds in the cabinets, and all sorts of chemicals and stuff for microscopy, not to speak of a nice fire in the grate and cups of tea floating around for occasional refreshers, my little room will be a real alchemist's den, won't it? Will you risk entering it? . . .

I mourn my neglect of poetry. Will the impulse ever return. My present mode of life does not conduce to it. The long days at Northbank and sense of leisure and space and of unhurried activities amid natural surroundings seem to be essential to me for expressing myself in verse. Others seem to find their inspiration in busier surroundings . . .

Kirkwall, 11 July 1961

My dear Ernest,

For two weeks I have been here in the office "at the receipt of custom", as they say. John[1] is south so I am keeping things together in the shop, pending his return (as I hope) next week when I hope to go to Westray for two weeks' holidays. I had made up my mind this year for a quiet solitary spell in the wilds . . .

I have got my garden in fair shape now, with tuberous begonias blooming in great style round the rose-bed. The roses, too, promise to flower well, though it is only their first year. Also, I have some wall-flower coming up for next year. All this has meant that I am appreciating very much the use of my summer-house, as it is very pleasant to look out on the garden from it. I am planning to make it a sort of laboratory-cum-greenhouse, and must fix up a work-bench in it, for handling specimens in preparation for making into microscope slides . . .

I spent a pleasant evening with Mr Groundwater[2] up at Stromness. We met in Birsay, where he was dismembering the whales for the Royal Scottish Museum. They were a rather rare species—Sowerby's Whale—a 'beaked' variety. Mother and daughter, both cast ashore in a storm, just below the Battery. He took me down to Stromness and showed me their School Exhibition. It was excellent and surpassed anything I have yet seen of the kind. The art section was a marvel, and shows that

SUMMER-HOUSE 'DAWNVALE'

their art teacher can not only himself paint but that he is a real teacher. Some of the paintings were most accomplished and mature in manner . . .

[1] John Laughton, Rendall's cousin and business partner in George Rendall & Co. After Robert Rendall's retiral he was sole partner. The business was eventually sold to the proprietor of J. & J. Smith, the drapery business formerly owned by Robert Rendall's Brethren Bible Class teacher, Charles Smith. George Rendall & Co., which had been founded in 1861, ceased trading in 1990 and the premises were acquired by The Leonards, the booksellers. This latter business had been owned by another of Rendall's early encouragers, George Leonard.

[2] William Groundwater (1906-1982), Rector of Stromness Academy and author of *Birds and Mammals of Orkney* (1974).

Kirkwall, [1961]

My dear Ernest,

9.30 p.m. Phewooo! I wipe my brow, having got my impedimenta for Westray wilds duly packed and ready for the steamer tomorrow morning. Three *huge* packages, a big suitcase and a fair-sized attache. Beach House[1] is in for a shock.

But first of all I was delighted to get your long and most interesting letter, and am so pleased that you are making such a good recovery. I was up a wee while beside Janette tonight, and I can see that she is looking forward very keenly to your quiet holiday together. If this good weather holds on you ought to have some new masterpieces in watercolour. We have been looking out the requisites etc.

How I wish you could have been with me tonight, to get a glimpse of my preparations for a lazy old-fashioned holiday. All I am taking with me (besides the usual togs for Sunday, fishing adventures, and lazing about in the sun) are a few things like my complete oil-painting outfit with 12 or so Daler Boards; my water-colour and charcoal tools, some tubes for shore specimens, only one of my seaweed presses (complete), some favourite books of verse, some books by Bridges on the theory of Miltonic prosody, six or seven big wooden models for some children's services, and other odds and ends, among them camera and tripod, with coloured films, a knapsack or two, a

Thermos, und so weiter, as the Deutschers would say. I am sure
that you will appreciate my baggage problem into the interior
of the wilds. Native labour is now very scarce, so perforce I
have to hire a car to come up for the luggage, and merely to
take the passenger as a sort of supernumerary. O aye, I have a
library of books with me, and Janette has topped them with one
of her favourite 'Devotionals'. Madam Guyon—Oh well, I
suppose I shall not be the worse of it.

Well, Ernest, I am quite excited over the prospect of being
in the isle of my forebears again. It is 26 years since I had a
really long holiday there. This time I hope to stay until 4th
August, so we shall both be back in Kirkwall within a week or
so of each other.

I had a great afternoon last Wednesday. It was pouring rain,
but my guests came up in a troop, Dr. & Mrs Honeyman,[2]
Stanley Cursiter, with wife and daughter, and the Sheriff. We
had a great time going over the shells, and the pictures on the
walls were carefully examined. Dr. & Mrs Honeyman were very
nice in the house—plain and homely, but alive. We had
afternoon tea and the Sheriff handed round the cups. It was 4.30
before they left, and seemingly it was considered a great
afternoon. I had a job to find chairs for them all, but they
seemed to like to wander about and catch their eye on anything
else that they could see . . .

You'll be interested to hear that Dr. Marwick is now
getting the publication of his work on the Birsay place-names
collected by Mr Sabiston, into print . . . It should be a work
comparable in value and interest with The Rousay Placenames
book.[3]

. . . SO, my spirit leaps to Grobist, where I hope to spend
a lazy afternoon tomorrow, with a book of verse—but not a cup
of wine—by my side.

Every blessing be yours in your holiday,

Yours affectionately
Robert

---

[1] A guesthouse in Westray.
[2] Dr T. J. Honeyman, Director of Glasgow Art Galleries and Museums.
[3] *The Place-names of Rousay* (1947). *The Place-names of Birsay* appeared
posthumously in 1970.

Monday after Easter
[Aberdeen, 1966]

My dear Ernest & Janette,

This is my first letter since before the operation— you are, of course, my local correspondents as well as my dear friends. Your last letter came this forenoon with all its news of developments in Kirkwall. Let me have a copy of George's poems won't you. Glad he is keeping *active*. Since my op. I have not been able to read my correspondence so I have a pile of letters to go through. Back here in Cornhill is fine & quiet & homely. The male nurses are very considerate & there are only a very few residents, quite private in fact . . . Then last Saturday afternoon I had such a nice visit from Prof Wynne Edwards & his wife who came in specially from their country cottage to see me, and brought a delightful bunch of various spring flowers. We had a *long* & mutually interesting talk. He is to publish my Orkney Hydroids & Polyzoa when I get well enough to tackle these. This will be some time yet as I am gathering strength very slowly. I have a good bit to catch up on from *5 stone 7 lbs*. Quite amazing—only skin & bone when I came here. But the Lord has been good . . .

Il Paradiso
Stromness
Saturday
[St Peter's House, 1966]

Dear Ernest,

I write this in our wee Writing Room—time 6.45 p.m. with the sun streaming in through the windows. The changing views of Scapa Flow over the town roofs are a continual delight. Living in a house like this gives one a real weather-sense—one of the basic things of life. I had it at Northbank but not at Dawnvale.

Sometime each day I manage down to the town, & keep in touch with the street. A car takes me up home—I have a good arrangement about this with Peace's garage. Last night the car took the route via Well Park so I stopped a moment & contacted George who has promised to come up some day: he was looking well. Also, one morning I saw Stanley Cursiter. I still hope to be down with him on Tuesday as he comes in the early afternoon & has assured me that I shall be home in good time— possibly in the evening. We shall likely see each other sometime but may not manage a prolonged contact. That will come later on as opportunity offers.

I'm getting the huddle of Stromness Lanes sorted out & learning the *easy* short cuts which avoid the steeper ups and downs. On the whole I am managing to move about but still get easily tired. Through the day I do fine, but at nights my sleep is *very* intermittent which makes me a bit dizzy in the mornings . . .

Today I got the full galley-proofs for The Hidden Land from the Orcadian Office. After reading these I find that besides several corrections I shall have to make one or two slight alterations . . .

What ploys have you on at the moment. You are having a busy but satisfying profession, but must not allow it to cause neglect of your personal literary interest. Time goes more quickly than we think! I wish I could do some Orkney Variants for Persian & Chinese Poems—the days here are *too short* & the congenial conditions tempt one to too much desultory reading.

Ever your friend & comrade
Robert

Stromness, 17 November 1966

My dear Ernest,

. . . Now I must return to your fairies. I have—imaginatively—had two experiences of fairydom. My first time in England, waking in the train in the early morning I looked out on a green English countryside, and lo, there was a fairy ring! It was like a welcome from the wee folks. The other occasion was in a narrow green dell in the hills near Edinburgh, where, under the short-cropped grass, I felt that I was treading on fairy territory. The impression was quite strong . . .

Stromness, 23 December 1966

My dear Ernest,

Our time seemed to go so quickly but I greatly enjoyed the few hours with you. Thanks for all your care and thought. And what shall I say about the delightful gift from Janette & yourself. Nothing could have been more acceptable—so, a big "Thank-you".

The School Concert was a great affair & the uniform excellence of the items on the Programme reflected great credit on the teachers. How much more comprehensive is education now than it was in our young days. The physical exercises were most interesting to watch, especially the 4 or 5 tier human pyramid which had various stages—cart-wheels etc. One young boy climbed the pyramid from outside and inside and bounced about like an india-rubber ball. Most fascinating! Then the rendering of Orkney verse was excellently done. Five items each of Edwin, George & myself. Carol singing, too, with items of instrumental music. After an interval we were given a rendering of the Gulling of Malvolio from the Twelfth Night. Great fun! The young folks pitched into it with abandon. I could follow each stage in mime—even though I could not catch the words. Altogether—a real Stromness occasion! But I must catch the post now. Sorry to trouble you yesterday but cousin John took over. It was for me a hectic afternoon—just two hours or so in with Jerry.[1]

A restful Christmas to you both.

Robert

[1] Gerald Meyer, editor of *The Orcadian* 1947-1983.

Stromness, 28 January 1967

My dear Ernest,

I'm not sure whose turn it is to write, but as this whole week has been spent indoors, except for this afternoon, and I have not been able, owing to a bout of flu with a chest cold and a bad stomach turn, to get my usual run to Kirkwall, I simply must send you a line to keep our correspondence up to date. I was kept in bed for four days in good comfort, and felt thankful

to be so well looked after. The doctor popped along twice to
see me. I think that the very severe weather has had something
to do with it.

But today my good friend Ian[1]—so *reliable*—took me a run
out to Yesnaby in the afternoon. We left about three o'clock
and I was duly installed (yes, that is the word) in the car with a
cosy tartan rug and A HOT-WATER BOTTLE. Did you ever!
So that while Ian went to paint a medium size canvas and
disappeared somewhere along the cliff-top, I read a book on art
in the comfort of the car. In little over an hour he returned
triumphantly with a completed cliff and sea picture. His
pictures, I think, show an increasing sense of harmony: that is,
they are not patchy in their execution but one sees at a first
glance 'the whole picture' and not just a good passage in it. And
you simply must come some day and see his portraits. He has
done one now of an old lady: it has a rich strong harmony of
colour, and the figure is not just painted as a figure in isolation
from its background. And he has caught both the resigned
tiredness of old age with its patient wisdom also . . .

Congratulations again on the excellence of your further
article in The Scots Magazine. I like the note of personal
experience in it which tones down what too often in such
articles becomes an unbroken series of historical allusions. The
Scots Magazine is a bit prone to this type of contribution. But
the human note gives proportion to such writing. You seem to
have gathered an immense amount of material about the 'past'.
The article in the Orcadian this week had much original matter.
I appreciate the historical research you have been doing in so
many directions regarding our Orkney life (shades of John
Mooney and Storer Clouston), but in your public writing you
must not neglect the imaginative (or should I say the literary?)
side of things. We do not get much of that now in The
Orcadian, do we?

I think I told you that Jeremy had been urging me to write
a paper for the Orcadian, but somehow I cannot get my mind
to concentrate upon it. I think the real reason is that I have
become obsessed again with poetry. I have been doing a good
deal of re-reading, and also browsing through critical books on
English prosody . . .

Of late I have been studying the effect of 'quantity' in verse
as distinct from 'accent'. Although English verse is largely
accentual, the position of long and short syllables in a single line

has much to do with its prosodial quality. A long vowel, for example, may fall upon an unaccented syllable in a particular foot, without breaking the accentual rhythm of the line, but a finer effect can be obtained when they are made to coincide . . .

My kind greetings to Janette: I hope that she is keeping in good health?

Ever your friend and comrade
Robert

[1] Ian MacInnes, local artist and principal art teacher, later Rector, of Stromness Academy.

Stromness, 7 March 1967

Dear Ernest,

As I did not manage to get into Kirkwall last week, and failed also to see you yesterday when in town, I must send you a wee friendly note—not that I have much to write about. The weather has been so severe that I have been kept mostly indoors . . .

Your much appreciated and thoughtful Christmas gift has been a real boon to me. At the moment, when in the mood, I am working at several literary projects. I've given priority to two:

(1) The History of the Orkney Antiquarian Society, with profiles of its members. This is taking shape not too badly, but I wish to work at it leisurely and make as good a job of it as I can. I feel that I ought to have it printed as an Orkney pamphlet after it has been used in the *Orcadian*. Newspaper files serve for research, but bury papers that should be readily available at any time in our home libraries. Don't you agree?

(2) I've been asked to make a personal contribution to a series now being run in *The Witness:* BOOKS THAT HAVE HELPED. In a very tame fashion I may put a friendly cat among the pigeons. The theme attracts me.

For the rest, I have in mind, as you know, the possibility (a very slight one) of getting a collection of my better poems published by Faber & Faber: A spiritual autobiography: A small handbook on the Epistle to the Hebrews: and in the far distance my very incomplete primary list of the Hydroids.[1] It is difficult to work at some of these projects away from my books and papers . . .

I hope that you continue to find pleasure in your various interests. What a pity you were not with me at Warbeth (in a car) on Thursday last week. The mountains of surging heaps of sea swinging through Hoy Sound was a picture that you would have wanted to photograph—the Hoy hills streaked with snow and seen under a veil of cloud 'real MacInnes' sky' made a perfect backcloth. Did I tell you that one day Ian took me up to Birsay and I showed him the magnificent painting possibilities of the North shore with Costa in middle distance and Rousay in the horizon? He has already done two big canvasses, one of them simply magnificent, but I rather think I must have mentioned this already to you. You simply must come up sometime so that we can both see Ian's work together.

Ever your devoted friend,
Robert

[1] Of this list, only the history of the O.A.S. was written.

TO WILLA MUIR

The novelist and translator Willa Anderson (1890-1970) was born in Montrose of Shetland parents. In 1919 she married the poet Edwin Muir (1887-1959). She and her husband collaborated on a number of projects including the translation of Kafka into English. Robert Rendall admired Edwin Muir's work and was influenced by it. Of Rendall's letters to the Muirs, only this letter to Willa Muir, written after Muir's death, survives.

Kirkwall, 29 September 1962

Dear Mrs Muir,

Ever since I acquired Edwin's *"Essays on Literature and Society"* (which I have had for some years and re-read from time to time) I have been captivated by his critical insights—so it was with extreme pleasure that I clapped eyes on his long-awaited

105

"The Estate of Poetry" and became its first purchaser in Orkney! Its contents delight me. They say so much what needs to be said in these days. The observations on 'audience' and 'public' match with my own feelings, possibly because of my own experience. My own verse has a happy Orkney 'audience' and I have always pitied those frustrated (and clever!!) poets in Edinburgh who find it so difficult to catch the ear of an amorphous & apathetic 'public'. I do not mind being provincial and have more satisfaction in my poems being used in our Orkney schools and enjoyed in farm houses than if they received fine critical reviews. This is true.

What Edwin has to say about reviewers scrutinising poems rather than experiencing them is very much to the point. When a boy and right through my youth I soaked myself in the delight of reading poetry and came into the experience of it like breathing. And I have never been able to shake off the thought that it was when I entered upon life in a croft at Northbank & shared in the orderly procession of the seasons in country work that I had a 'return' to the writing of verse—first finding fruition in "Country Sonnets" and later in Orkney Variants. My contact with Edwin deepened my sensibility in several ways and influenced *to a considerable extent* my later poems in "Orkney Shore Poems". Since then I have written few poems but it looks as if I may have a happy period again. Next January I hope to retire from business and—just fancy it!—become an old age pensioner. Can you believe it?

Rather over a year ago I wrote you a long letter, carried it in my pocket until it became dog-eared, and then did not post it—a foolish but characteristic habit of mine. I had wished to send you a copy of my "Orkney Shore" and now renew my

PIEROWALL
WESTRAY

desire. So if you have not read it, it would give me great pleasure to send you a copy—let me know, won't you? It received kind reviews—especially one in The Glasgow Herald under Prof. C. M. Yonge's name. The Times Lit rather looked down their nose at it but I didn't mind that, as one of my favourite pastimes is to read their Letters to the Editor in which authors aggrieved by reviews protest in a pained voice against unfair reviewing. The consequent battle of wits (done *so* politely) can be very amusing. The book itself might have been better but I intended it for a mixture of mercies. After all a certain wise lady said to me "Never mind the facts—what we want to see is Robert!"

I hope you keep in comfortable health. Ernest gives me news from time to time. He is now taking his book on Orkney Social History seriously once more and has got the first two chapters done. I keep pegging away at him about it. He now keeps in wonderful health. You will know that Prof. Butter was in Orkney in connection with his projected life of Edwin. It was a busy time & I did not see him. But he wrote me & I allowed him to copy one or two of Edwin's letters. I hope that I did right in this?

I've now got a *good* Stereoscopic Binocular microscope and am working on our Orkney Hydroids and Polyzoa. A Research Vessel was up recently & brought me 9 sacks dredged material to examine.

With my love & regards
Robert

TO WILLIAM TRAILL

William Traill (1864-1944) came from an old family of Orkney lairds. He was a civil engineer, and in his youth he had worked on the construction of the Forth Bridge. After his retirement, he settled at Holland House, Papa Westray, the ancestral home of the senior branch of the family. Traill had a great love of all things Orcadian, and built up a private collection of antiquities, fine art and books. After they first met in the late 1920s, Traill encouraged Robert Rendall in his archaeological and natural history studies. Traill was strong and forthright in his opinions, and Rendall delighted in his company, later devoting a chapter of

Orkney Shore *to a description of him. He conducted his own archaeological exploration at the Knap of Howar in Papa Westray, and it was his discoveries there which occasioned these letters from Rendall.*

Kirkwall, 18 March 1936

Dear Mr Traill,

I have just returned from my trip south, arriving here by plane on Monday. Although my time away was filled with business activities, I found time to squeeze in a number of personal interests.

In the second-hand bookstalls I picked up several very useful books on Conchology, Woodward's manual with hundreds of figures of recent and fossil Mollusca for 8d., a single volume of Jeffrey's British Conchology for 1/-, a catalogue of the Mollusca of the Firth of Clyde (more recent than the well-known British Association Report on the fauna of the same area).

In Edinburgh I called upon Dr A. C. Stephen,[1] and was glad to learn that a thorough and scientific Faunistic survey of Scotland is now in progress, and that the results are to be fully published. In connection therewith Dr Stephen and a colleague are to visit Orkney this Spring, and upon my advice are to work the Birsay area for marine forms.

While in Glasgow I had a full report on your Knap o' Howar flints. This is rather too long to copy out in extenso, but I shall copy out the more interesting parts. Shall I send you the letter for perusal, or will you be in town sometime soon?

> With the exception of 11 Flakes and scrapers, the flints show no signs whatever of having been fractured by blows stuck by man . . . fractures point to frost and thermal action and possibly crushing as well. The 5 flakes show secondary or tertiary flaking . . . the scrapers show much use . . . as regards the period it is regretted that there is nothing whatever by which one can tell to what culture the specimens belong. As specimens of implements they are extremely poor, but as examples of artefacts worked in the simplest way possible they are scientifically very interesting. Their importance will exist in their being kept with all the other relics that may be found at the

Knap. Separated from these, they can only interest the student of Orkney stone industries.

From the foregoing you will see that the small collection is not without special interest, and subject to your permission I would be pleased to prepare a short paper on them for our Society. Mr Lacaille[2] had given me a detailed technical report on the individual flints which, accompanied by an illustration, would be of definite value in our proceedings, and could be used by Mr Kirkness in his more general paper for Edinburgh.[3]

With kind regards,

Yours sincerely,

Robert Rendall

---

[1] Assistant Keeper, later Keeper, of Natural History at the Royal Scottish Museum, Edinburgh.

[2] The archaeologist, an authority on the Scottish Mesolithic period, who had given Rendall a report on Traill's flints. He also gave Rendall reports on the South Ettit flints.

[3] William Kirkness F.S.A.Scot. (1886-1974), a teacher and practitioner of traditional crafts, helped Traill at the Knap of Howar. He and Traill wrote a paper on the site, 'Howar, a Prehistoric structure on Papa Westray, Orkney', in *Proc. Soc. Antiq. Scot.*, 71 (1936-7).

RENNIBISTER EARTH-HOUSE

109

H

Kirkwall, 27 March 1936

Dear Mr Traill,

I received your welcome letter, and am pleased to know that you consider Mr Lacaille's report satisfactory. Of course I should not think of utilising this material without first obtaining the unqualified approval of William Kirkness and yourself. In the meantime I am retaining the second batch of your flints until I get the South Attit collection made up for sending to Lacaille for a detailed report. This may not be for several weeks but I have your batch laid by in a safe place. Later on, in the event of my having to prepare a paper on the flints from Howar, I should have to make a special drawing of the more important for purposes of reproduction.

While in Banff, I visited the local collection, and was annoyed to find that Edward's collection is mouldering away into absolute decay,[1] and that there is no local interest in either natural history or in archaeology—so much for *Municipal* Museums which are not associated with a live Society. We ought to have a strong Society control in *our* Museum, and I intend to keep my personal contributions *on loan,* lest a degenerate public body should led the whole museum 'go to pot'. Banff to me was a warning.[2]

I saw Edward's house, and had a chat with a shoemaker, whose workshop is connected with the house in which the famous Scottish naturalist followed the same calling. His name however is not cherished by the townspeople as it might be. Among the working classes he is remembered as a man who would not attend to his work, as, in fact lazy, a man who would not work. Such is the blindness of invincible ignorance!

Since returning to Kirkwall, I have been kept busy with commercial interests, and getting prepared for our Spring trade. This has left little time for other things. In this issue of the Conchological Journal, there is an interesting report by Professor Boycott on the *Neritina* found in the waters of the Loch of Stenness. This is its only station in Scotland, and it is interesting to know that the water is exactly the same in salinity *and in the proportion of lime* as in the English and Irish localities, and that there are very few places with similar conditions in the North of Scotland. This fixes a definite habit on the part of the mollusc.

Now I must run to the shop.

With kind regards,

Yours sincerely,
Robert Rendall

---

[1] Thomas Edward (1814-1886), Banff shoemaker and naturalist, noted for his detailed zoological observations and his study of crustaceans. Edward was largely unappreciated in Banff, and his collection, which included archaeological artefacts, has deteriorated badly. There is a biography by Samuel Smiles, *Life of a Scotch Naturalist, Thomas Edward* (1876).

[2] Marginal note: 'I saw the *'auld been'*, however, the subject of so much controversy between Edward & the authorities on prehistoric remains.' The 'auld been' (old bone) was thought by Edward—mistakenly it is now known—to be that of a plesiosaur.

TO JOHN R. WATSON

While Robert Rendall was working on the biography of Joseph B. Watson, editor of **The Witness,** *a correspondence grew up between him and Watson's son, John R. Watson (b.1919), then living in Berkhamsted. In the following extracts, which show the various stages of the book's writing, he reflects on the nature of composition and gives John Watson the flavour of his life in Orkney. John Watson visited Rendall when he was in hospital in Aberdeen, and the letter Rendall wrote once he was back in Orkney is also included.*

Kirkwall, 18 March 1956

My dear John,

I was on the point of posting your card yesterday when your second packet of material reached me. I was glad to have your letter with its suggestions, and am comforted to think that I shall have your counsel and support in my part of our common task. Until full documentation has been sent me I do not intend beginning to write the biographical section of the book. Later on I shall send you a full questionnaire on points upon which I shall require more information. In the meantime what eggs you have sent me are in the nest and are being incubated. I find that if, after digesting *facts,* these are left to simmer[1] in the mind, a day comes when they can be dealt with rapidly in writing and a definite pattern assumed. Then the result can be laid aside until the excitement of writing dies down, and afterwards given cool criticism. This takes TIME. So that, while on the one hand I am anxious to accede to the desire to have the work done at as early a date as possible, on the other I do not intend to spoil it by over-hasty thinking or over-hasty writing. I have accepted the task as coming from the Lord, and He does not over-drive His servants. But I am so pleased that you are sending me all the material as you are doing, as now I am beginning to get a good overall idea of what shape the book is likely to take . . .

[1] Note in margin: 'simmering after digestion!!!'

Kirkwall, 2 October 1956

Dear John,

Here am I, by the fire, the curtains drawn, and the tangled MASS of my papers before me. The other day I went through a fat file of your father's letters (to ME), and took down extracts that are going to be useful, since I understand the context in which they were written. Also I have gathered my bricks into heaps, diary bricks, correspondence bricks, magazine bricks, and have begun to build the wall of the house. Our waiting time has not been lost time for a builder can do little until the architect has completed his PLAN. I am now beginning to see my way ahead . . .

Now forgive me, I must go and watch your father as a boy, having finished his sums in the classroom, mischievously so tying the other boys' legs to their seats that when these were asked to rise they could not! But cheer up, we shall not leave him there!

My love to you all
Robert

Kirkwall, 5 April 1957

My dear John,

The morning sun is pouring in through the front window: my tame blackbird is sitting contentedly on her nest above the front door; the bushes in the garden are each showing their characteristic colour scheme of greens into russets; and I sit here heaving a sigh of relief that our great task is reaching harbour at long last. Everything now seems to be set fair for publication. Enough of that for a minute or two. Let us take a deep breath.

The blackbird? She is a beauty, and has been roosting all winter on the edge of the lintel, right against the glass of the fanlight above the door—quite undisturbed by door-bangings and flutter of people and visitors. I have a talk with her every morning and she casts down a kindly eye upon her friend. Two years ago she tried to build a nest in the same place, but it kept toppling over. In the end, after I had put up a strip of wood to help her, she laid eggs, but another blackbird intruder came and they had a fight, which ended in the eggs being knocked out of the nest and smashed. This year there has been no breach of the peace. She lets me come within an inch or so of her, and only if I put up my hand too near does she fly out: even then she waits for a good while before rising. Great, isn't it?

This week the staff photographer of The Scottish Field was along and I got him to take a close up picture of her: I expect that he will use it in the autumn sometime—in the magazine. My nose was nearly in the nest!

You'll have seen my hymn[1] in this month's 'Witness' (with its one printer's error!). It was written on the 30th December between 1 a.m. and 6 a.m. Last night I heard it sung for the first time in a choir practice in one of our large local churches, where it is to be sung as an Easter Hymn next Sunday. I won't be there, but the choir-master—an old school-mate of mine— very kindly asked me along to hear them practising it. Two verses are being sung as solos, one by a male voice the other by a lady: other two, one by all the men, the other by the ladies; one verse by the whole choir, the remainder by congregation and choir. I am very pleased that its first public use should be in my home town and among my own people . . .

[1] 'The Trial'.

Sometime in October
[Birsay, 1957]

Dear John,

I am in retreat at Birsay for a few days after a spell of weeks in which I have been kept more active one way and another than the natural tempo of my mind—already fast enough—cares to move. Today I have been *'sleeping out'* my mental staleness— congenially enough, too, for outside my cottage window rain darkens the sky and the raging line of Atlantic breakers shows white against the low cloud. The postman brought me a copy of Berkouwer's 'The Triumph of Grace in the Theology of Karl Barth'. I've been dipping into it and at the same time enjoying a leisurely cup of afternoon tea with cookie & jam . . .

BURNMOUTH, BIRSAY c1960

Stromness, 12 August 1966

My dear John & Gwynnith,

Here I am, domiciled in dear old Orkney, though not, as I might have hoped, in Kirkwall. Though much improved in health I still need medical supervision and the doctors have arranged for me to stay in this delightful modern-equipped Eventide Home which is high on a hillside overlooking the town & over toward the hills of Hoy. Scapa Flow is spread out in front. I have been given a room of my own which ensures a measure of privacy (much appreciated) though there are rest rooms, quiet room, writing room and various wee nooks with comfortable arm chairs. "Alcoves" for auld coves! is how I put it.

I can see the Lord's hand in my present circumstances. The leading brother here[1] died a few weeks ago & left a bare ½ dozen to carry on—so I hope to be a wee help to them. I am not very mobile yet but I have been able to make an arrangement with a local Garage for transport when I need it.

I look back with great pleasure to your visit at Cornhill. It warmed my heart to have your company for a whole day. Cecil[2] has written me from time to time & has accepted both my poem on Bees[3] and also a short article on Heb. 13. "He hath said, I will never leave thee, nor forsake thee!" Did I tell you that I had a visit from Geoffrey Bull?[4]

My brother Willie & his wife, along with their son Bertie & his wife & family are north for a short holiday. I am getting leave to stay with them in Kirkwall for a few days in my own house there.

I am hoping to have a small volume of poems published before Christmas—20pp. printed locally. My 4th volume of verse.

The other week I had a letter from the Oxford University Press, asking permission to use two of my poems in their forthcoming Oxford Book of Scottish Verse. Both are dialect poems—one of them in the ancient Scaldic measure.

Let me have all your home news when you have leisure to write.

Ever affectionately yours

Robert

---

[1] The small Brethren congregation in Stromness.
[2] Cecil Howley, editor of *The Witness*.
[3] 'On the Cross', *The Witness* 96 (Nov., 1966), p. 408. The poem is a meditation on Ps 118:12, 'They compassed me about like bees.'
[4] A Brethren itinerant preacher.

SELECTED PROSE
OF
ROBERT RENDALL

PIEROWALL, WESTRAY c.1915

THE LITERARY USES OF DIALECT

While working on his dialect poetry, Robert Rendall began studying dialect and its literary uses. He evidently intended to write an essay on the subject but this never got beyond some fragmentary notes, probably made about 1947. They reflect the literary debates of the time. Hugh MacDiarmid and his literary followers had experimented with a Scots vocabulary that was partly taken from Scottish literature or historical dictionaries and partly taken from Scots idioms still in use. It was this vocabulary that James Fergusson had disparagingly called 'plastic Scots' in a radio broadcast in 1946. Like Fergusson, Rendall disapproved of the way the use of Scots had been made into a literary shibboleth, but he agreed with Douglas Young's viewpoint that great lyricists, such as Burns, were eclectic in their language use and forged a vocabulary out of what language was available to them from their reading and from their society.

Being an Orcadian gave Rendall, as it did Edwin Muir, a different perspective on the debate over Scots—in Orkney both English and Scots were languages of invading cultures. He felt that there was little point in trying to turn the clock back: English was now the dominant language in Britain, and Scots had been relegated to a language variant (as he defined dialect). Mac-Diarmid's use of Scots had been part of his attempt to express a modern Scottish consciousness and avoid the sentimentality of the Kailyard. Rendall, too, wanted to avoid 'kailyardism' and he felt that dialect, in the places where it survived, preserved the disappearing modes of life and thought that were under threat from the dominant culture. In capturing these, he thought, there was a place for dialect poetry. This edited version of Rendall's notes provides an insight into his mind while he was working on the poems of **Orkney Variants.**

119

The Shorter Oxford Dictionary defines dialect as 'a variant of a living language'. Such variants may be due to fragmentary survivals of an earlier speech or to developed local usage, most probably to both. The replacement of one language by another is not sudden and formal, but takes place gradually over a more or less extended period of time. Old habits of thought persist, and speech-forms that have no exact equivalent in the superceding language refuse to be jettisoned and survive as idiomatic dialect-words or sentence structure. When a local vernacular is rich in such survivals, there is a field for dialect poetry. In addition, old speech habits affect the use of the new language and create turns in syntax, over-riding standard usage. This is frequently observed in the spoken English of a Gaelic-thinking people, frequently made the butt of English humour, but nothing to be ashamed of. The same thing holds good in phonetics. Peculiarities in pronunciation rise from the trans-ference of old vowel inflections to imperfectly heard words in the new tongue; or it may be that some inability to frame a new sound may result in the persistence of a cognate old one, as it still is with some Orcadians who pronounce quarry as 'wharry' and quarrel as 'wharrel', simply because the 'q' sound was not used in Old Norse.

A people's literature includes the written word in all its forms: prose, poetry, private letters, diaries, law documents, public newspapers, and also, one must now suppose, govern-ment publications. Being addressed to a nation-wide community it employs a common language-medium; in our land, standard English. Literature, to be an effective means of communicating thought and feeling, or even to serve the ends of propaganda, must conform to the language habits of the people addressed. While this may mean on occasion the use of dialect, a national literature, if it is to flow in the main current of a people's life and not lose itself in academic backwaters, must run in the channel scooped out by actual historical circumstance. Whether we like it or not, and without prejudice to what survives in the vernacular of the old Scots tongue, writing is now, in Scotland as in England, conducted in English. Whatever privileges Scottish poetry may stake out for itself against the dominance of English in other fields of literature, it cannot afford to ignore or belittle as a means of poetic communication a language that is now so closely interwoven into the general life of the community and which has proved a noble instrument in the hands of acknowledged Scottish poets. And it ought not to be overlooked that the superscription 'Poems in Scots', so frequently used by poets themselves Scotsmen, infers that 'Scots' no longer holds its place as a national language. What would be said if an English poet laureate were to entitle his collected works 'Poems in English'!

English has long been the common denominator of vernacular speech. Scots, once a language in its own right, does not now even exist side by side with English, as does Gaelic, but survives only in a context of common English, and thus in some sense has become a dialect form. Much the same thing took place in Orkney with regard to the old native speech, the Orkney Norn, a distinct branch of the old West Scandinavian group of tongues, and which persisted in the islands as a language in its own right, down into the middle of the eighteenth century. But eventually it was superceded by Scots, which in the process became modified, through local usage. But in the end Scots prevailed, though old native idioms refused to be suppressed, and a rich vocabulary of Old Norse words persisted in the common speech in much the same way as words in braid Scots now enrich a Scottish vernacular based on English. Scots in turn gave place to English, and as Orcadians from their Norse traditions and remembrance of oppression under Scottish earls hold no brief for purely Scottish interests, this may partly account why Orcadian writers use English without inhibitions. While quietly tenacious of their old Norse heritage, they are too well aware of cultural values of English literary tradition, and of Scots, to despise either, and gladly strike fresh roots into the rich soil of both. Orcadians, while quietly tenacious of old ways, are too well aware of their own interests to jettison literary plunder from other lands or to refuse whatever flotsam and jetsam of words and language the tides of history may cast up on their shores. Many an old house in Orkney was raftered with the ribs of stranded 'foreign' ships, and yet thatched with native heather. Historical development cannot be ignored. The island vernacular today becomes increasingly conformed to standard English, but there still survives, especially in the remoter districts, words and idioms from the old language flavoured by Scottish elements.

Dialect, then, is local in its genius. It is a manuscript of local history as language is of national history, and preserves the peculiarities of local development. For this reason interest in dialect has always been a mark of local piety. But over and above such survivals of ancient speech-habits there is another factor that must be taken into account when seeking to account for dialect. Alien usages are naturalised, and in the process frequently acquire a local character. New words introduce themselves, whose original meaning, imperfectly apprehended, suffers change; and a new, though cognate meaning, supplants the old. This has not infrequently taken place in Orkney with regard to Scots words.

The 'local' character of dialect makes it undesirable to throw particular dialects into a common melting-pot and expect a new national language to emerge. The result can only be an artificial and arbitrary conglomerate such as Esperanto. Yet the instinct that seeks to save dialect from extinction is sound. How is this to be done? Is it possible to create a genuine though limited 'literature' within the framework of a wider national tradition? So that it will at once reflect a local culture and be integrated with a broader literary development? And if so, what are the literary uses of dialect?

William Barnes, the dialect poet of Dorsetshire, speaks of writing "in what some may deem a fast out-wearing speech-form" and as "writing one's name in the snow of a spring day"; a feeling shared by Robert Louis Stevenson when he spoke of his Scots poems as written in "a dying language". Local piety lingers round declining native tradition, and seeks to preserve in memory the last accents and vital glances of ancestral heritage. Sentiment therefore not infrequently ousts sober judgment, and only when a firm grip is kept on sensibility do poetical expressions of feeling have literary distinction. Poems in the vernacular live when they are actual transcripts of contemporary life; when, though they may characterise a fast-disappearing communal life, they are shot through with the timeless and elemental in human experience, as in Violet Jacob's 'Tam i' the Kirk'. But the margin between this superlative use of the vernacular and excessive sentimentality is so thin, even in the work of a single poet, that few seem able always to keep on the safe side of the line. Simplicity of diction seems essential, since such communities as are depicted in dialect are usually unsophisticated and direct in their speech; which, however, does not connote lack of intelligence or character. Consistency requires that such dialect poems should not introduce into the mouth of its subjects words and idioms now alien to their normal speech-habits. The instinctive usages of the common people (Wordsworth was right here), the living, even if declining, tradition enshrined in a sensitive native vernacular, provide the medium through which contemporary life in a particular locality can best find expression. True, the result, in the hands of an indifferent craftsman, may well be 'kailyardism' and may rarely rise above the level of the provincial newspaper, and therefore in the strictest sense not be literature. But even so, if it is sincerely wrought and faithfully reflects local life it may, without making high pretentions, serve a worthy end.

HARVEST OF BERE

At the beginning of World War II Robert Rendall bought a small croft, Northbank, in Scapa. He wanted to experience country life, and he did most of the farm work himself. In doing this he was influenced by the descriptions of pastoral life in Classical poetry. It is characteristic of his return to the land that he should grow a crop of bere. Bere, four-rowed barley, has been found in Neolithic tombs in Orkney, and for centuries it had been one of the staple crops of the islands, providing both food and malt. Although its hardiness made it suitable for the uncertain climate of Orkney, it was fairly coarse, and by the twentieth century it had been largely replaced by crops with greater commercial potential such as oats or the finer two-row barley. As Rendall found out, this created problems when it came to threshing and grinding the bere. This description of his first harvest appeared in **The Glasgow Herald** *in February 1949. It was also the subject of his poem 'Winter Threshing'.*

The harvest that year was late, and strong winds had flattened the crops, so that cutting had in many instances to be done with the scythe. Heavy rains, too, had made the fields unfit for the binder, or even the reaper. On my own small croft, which I had but lately acquired—largely as a result of reading Horace and Virgil!—and which I had cultivated with a beginner's earnestness during the earlier part of the season, there was a crop of bere.

123

That crop was the pride of my new way of life. Had I not seen it sown? Had I not, on a fine spring morning with the sun still low in the sky, caught the first green flush of the braird? And had not my own hands broadcast on the field a generous supply of fertiliser? It is but fair to add that interested neighbours afterwards remarked, "Boy, thoo'll lay the crop wi' all that manure!" Afterwards, note, as is the country fashion, not before: that would be interfering! But the bere grew, thick and high, the first field of this particular crop that had been seen in the district for some years, oats having supplanted the old-fashioned 'corn', or bere, from which the Orkney bere-bannock is made. I had been determined to grow and mill my own bere.

Strong winds came when the crop was about to form the full ear. Many were the slow prophetic head-shakings at this stage, but the growing crop confounded them all by completing its development before the heads got 'laid', when such growth would have been retarded if not altogether hindered. Jubilant after this near escape, the corn grew steadily on and ripened beautifully, the golden beards of the barley waving in the wind rhythmically and triumphantly. Alas, the high winds of our Orkney autumn played havoc with the exposed field and left the corn in a tangle. Only by scythe could the crop be cut.

Others were too busy with their own difficulties to give any assistance, so I perforce had to do what all scything experts must at one time have done—make a beginning. I bought a scythe. Enthusiastically if not scientifically the field was cut, and with the help—and inevitable advice, to which I listened respectfully—of a friendly neighbour the sheaves in due course were built on the headlands of the field in small stacks or 'disses', through which a drying wind could still further 'cure' the crop.

December came, with thoughts of threshing, but I found that there was no mill in the district that could thresh bere, the riddles of the mills being suited only for oats. But with a sheet of old flat mahogany from a cabinetmaker in the town (plywood being almost unobtainable in war-time), a brace and bit, and a red-hot poker, a new riddle was made in the evenings by the side of the peat-fire. On a cold clear December afternoon we carted the sheaves to the barn: they filled the loft to the peak of the rafters, and left only a small tunnel through which one could creep to the feeding-box of the mill.

At the time of building the stacks, several small 'windlins', or roughly twisted bundles of field-rakings, had been thrust into the heart of the stacks. These I now carried in huge armfuls into a corner of the barn for future hen-feeding, and, as I did so, felt a curious tickling of straw about my neck. This was repeated several times, but I thought no more on the matter, until, when forking up sheaves, I again felt that curious tickle at the back of my neck. I gave a rough brush with my hand, but this time my fingers closed on the snout of an animal—it had been there all the time.

My grip was insecure, and I was well-nigh demented to think that it might slip, and the mouse, or whatever it was, escape again into the security of my shirt. I held on. Amid much hilarity and laughter my cousin slowly undid the neckband of my shirt, while another friend stood ready to grasp the creature. They need not have troubled, for it was dead as a stone, its skull crushed by the pincer grip of my thumb and forefinger. It was a fine specimen of the Orkney vole—Microtis Orcadensis—which by way of requital I had stuffed and set up by a local taxidermist: thereafter it adorned the ben-end mantel-shelf as a memento of my first harvest.

Later in the evening I stood in the field of a neighbouring farm belonging to my uncle[1], and was relating to him my experience with the field-vole. I had just reached the climax of the story and was putting up my hand to demonstrate how it happened, when lo, to my horror I felt another. By this time I was frantic, for it was at least a couple of hours since the capture of the first. My uncle, normally a quiet and undemonstrative man, collapsed into uncontrollable laughter. It was several seconds before I realised that behind me had been standing, in full view of my uncle, that same merry-minded cousin who had 'rescued' me from the first vole, and who now, with a suitable bit of straw, had provided the second at the appropriate point in the story. Such are country ways!

More such rustic skylarking took place in the barn during the evening's threshing, when neighbours had gathered in to help, or perhaps, more accurately, to pass an interesting evening. But there was an atmosphere of good fellowship in work. One carted away mountainous heaps of straw as bedding for his cattle, another kept his eye on the sacks as they slowly filled from the hoppers, another tied them up and lifted them to the wall, still another raked down the rising clouds of straw, while one pawky experienced old farmer, watching with shrewd observant eye and thoroughly enjoying himself, caustically passed comments on how everything was being done.

I myself handled the sheaves, loosing the band, and setting the sheaf handy for my cousin, now serious-faced enough, for he was a great worker and was feeding the mill vigorously and had no time for banter. But throughout the threshing I kept my eye fixed on the whitewashed gable-end of the barn where great fantastic shadows waved their arms and strode about in strange figures as the men in the barn below moved between the wall and the oil-lantern that hung from one of the lower beams of the loft.

There was a continual hum from the mill, punctuated by angry gusts and by the occasional murmur of human voices. The atmosphere vibrated with dry dust whirled about by the energy and commotion of the mill. Sight, sound, and feeling combined to induce a strange sense of phantasmagoria, as if the spirits of the daedal earth had once again visited the haunts of men and given them the intoxication of primal things. But over all was the content of a season's work reaching its goal, and the assurance that I would eat my own bere-bannocks for the first time in my life.

[1] William Laughton of Foveran, father of John Laughton, the cousin mentioned earlier.

126

ITALY, 1950

Robert Rendall visited Italy for the first time in 1950. At the time the country was undergoing reconstruction and rapid industrial and economic expansion. In these selections from **Extracts from a Travel Diary** *(1950) he describes his first glimpses of Italy from the train, his arrival in Florence, and also his first visit to Pesaro on the Adriatic. In the Second World War Pesaro suffered heavily from Allied bombing, being at the eastern end of the Gothic Line, the defensive position taken up by the German Army in the winter of 1944-5 during its final defence of Italy. Fortunately, the town's older buildings escaped destruction, and despite the rebuilding, Pesaro retained its old character. Its museum has the largest collection in Italy of Majolica ware, a highly decorated tin-glazed pottery, and the town has long been an important centre for its production. Rendall became close friends with the Christian Brethren missionaries in Pesaro, Tom and Beatrice Harding. He enjoyed the company of the fishermen of the port and the farmers in the large rural hinterland around the town. Pesaro became the place where he felt most at home in Italy.*

April 28.   Awoke at 6 a.m. to see the Alps with cold morning sunlight gleaming on their snowy peaks, but mountainside and valley frosted over and lying in gloomy shadow. A few short tunnels take us to the Italian frontier, and into the full morning sunshine.

The landscape from now on has fresh interest. The train winds its way through valleys terraced with vineyards or plunges through gorges connecting narrow valley with narrow valley. We have glimpses of peasant-women, with grey head-shawls, leading mules in small walled enclosures difficult of cultivation; others hack away at the clods or rake the broken soil. A butterfly dances past. Trees are in full foliage, and orchards in blossom.

Mountainside villages, beyond normal modes of road transport, retain characteristic grey-slated roofs, weathered and lichened, and blending fitly with the landscape; but as the valleys widen out and small towns begin to appear, mass-production and uniformity show themselves in rows of red-tiled ridges. Many of the valley river-beds are flat, dry channels, gleaming white in the sunshine, but where water appears it is that blue-green water peculiar to the mountains.

Unfamiliar details of agricultural life catch the eye. Bundles of tree-prunings remind one of the careful husbandry of the peasant: they will serve as plant-props, and also for making fences (reminiscent of the Orkney 'flackie'[1]). A woman is seen washing clothes in the river-bed. Others are spreading dung in field-drills. Some hay-fields are cut. This is the valley life, but perched fantastically away up on the heights are cultivated patches that testify how the people live between two worlds—that of the valley-meadows, and that of the mountain-alp.

We enter the Plain of Lombardy with its conical hills and big flattened knowes crowned with silhouette of houses. Our flautist[2] is now tootling away in a subdued meditative vein, completely lost to the company. The sun is getting really warm, and we realise that we are now south of the Alps.

Field-colours, which among the mountains were the dirty white of sun-baked clods, now take on vivid colours of reddish gold. Farm-wells, with long swing-poles, on which hang dangling buckets, invite a sketch.

We reach Genoa and the Mediterranean. The city, seen from the train, is interesting architecturally, being a complex of solid blocks of flats, green-shuttered, a jumble of oblong planes of stucco—in yellow, pink, flame, and green—that almost justifies the vagaries of Cubist art. There are also newly-built flats and miniature sky-scrapers that add a distinctive note to the medley of buildings.

All colours are strong in the sunlight, and one wonders how Orkney artists, who see such colour in our grey northern isles, would blazon their canvasses in this southern sunshine. Certainly Van Gogh is no eccentric here, but a sober realist!

The Riviera! The much belauded territory of the idle rich! If sunshine, and palm-trees, and the blue Mediterranean, and elegant splendour in hotels, and dilettante living make up life's 'summum bonum', without doubt it can be found here, but as I look down on the tame beaches with all their facilities for boating and bathing and lounging in the sun, I say to myself, "Not a patch on Birsay!" Or was it that the sun was too hot?

We pass a small boat-building place, which retains evidence of precision bombing. The succession of short tunnels through Mediterranean bluffs and headlands becomes monotonous, and it is with relief that we turn inland towards Pisa.

The countryside explodes with vegetables and fruit-trees,

and again recalls Van Gogh—though miles away from Arles.

The vitality of the earth, supplemented by the industry of man, creates a marvellous picture of riotous growth, far removed from the slow sedate progress of crops in our Orkney fields.

If my borrowed Baedeker had not already primed me to look out for the Carrara quarries, which gleam white on the distant mountainside beyond this fertile plain, I should have had their existence forced on my attention by the huge blocks of marble, some rough-hewn, some more finely-dressed, that lie piled up by the side of the railroad. But these famous quarries hold less interest than the living panorama of country life that now passes before me.

In swift succession I see a water-cart yoked to two cream-coloured bullocks, scarlet poppies in the crops, straw-flackies set up tentwise to provide shelter for chickens from the sun, flocks of sheep complete with shepherdesses, pigs in small enclosures, hay ricks cut around in Italian fashion till they look like the stumps of half-eaten apples, with the central pole taking the place of the stem, numerous unfamiliar wild-flowers, and fruit-trees set in rows 20 feet or so apart, inter-planted with all manner of crops and irrigated by regular ditches. Everywhere colour continues violent. A peasant woman walks along a field path, black bundle on head.

My first sight of Pisa! Look, there is the domed Baptistery, the Cathedral front, the world-famous Leaning Tower (more properly, the Campanile), gleaming white in the sun.

It is not often that dreams of boyhood come true, but this one has. It's an Event! Which I duly celebrate in a diminutive tumbler of strong coffee, costing 40 lire, bought on the platform while changing trains for Florence. The small pottery tumbler will make a fine memento!

Shattered houses show how badly Pisa suffered in the last war. Demolished buildings gaze with eyeless sockets on the green landscape and gape vacantly on life. But soon we leave these behind. Florence comes in sight. Yes, yonder is Brunelleschi's Dome and Giotto's tower, familiar through long acquaintance by way of book-illustrations.

I recall the time when first, as a boy, I opened the pages of *The Children's Encyclopaedia* in Victoria Street, saw the picture of Giotto dreaming of his famous tower, and resolved to see that tower before I died. Now I have done it.

The sensation is repeated when, on reaching Florence and threading my way through the animated crowds that fill the streets, I suddenly come upon the Tower with its delicately coloured marbles muted in the lamplight and rising heavenward like a glorious dream in the very heart of a bustling city.

The Florentine tramcars beat the New Year's day ba'.[3] There is a rush to enter them, and the last few passengers cling desperately to precarious hand-grips along the sides of the tram, and have to shrink close in to avoid passing traffic. Evidently it is a game well understood, and played with accepted risks!

We reach the home of my Italian friends which is situated near a riverside on the edge of the city, high up below Fiesole. I slept soundly.

May 9. . . . I reach my destination—Pesaro, the birthplace of Rossini, and the town where Bernardo Tasso lived, many of whose classical sonnets were translated into English in the early years of the last century by James Glassford of Dougalston.

After the rich architectural splendour of Florence and Perugia, Pesaro at first sight seems undistinguished and, culturally, somewhat of a backwater. A car-run along the sea-front, however, reveals a fascinating old-fashioned harbour life. A long promenade also, complete with Lido, proclaims Pesaro a seaside resort, but happily it is too early in the season for the Blackpool crowds!

Factories give evidence of industrial interests and an open-air market promises near-by peasant country. So that if a historical and cultural background is lacking in the outward appearance of the town (unless a balcony where Mussolini gave one of his more belligerent speeches is taken into account) this is more than compensated for by the varied and picturesque community life.

Tomorrow, I shall explore the town.

May 10. Immediately after breakfast I walk down to the sea-front: on the way, from a little shop near the fish-market, I buy a bag of cherries, costing only 13 lire (about 2d).

Pesaro harbour, badly bombed in the war but now being repaired, covers a considerable area. Quays enclose a commodious "basin" filled this morning with Adriatic fishing vessels.

A few boys are casting handlines, with the same hope

Pesaro 12·5·50

though with rather less success than the young sillock-fishers at our Corn Slip. One or two older lads attempt the net.

At the end of the main quay is a yard for boat-building and repair; several large vessels fill the stocks by the slipway. These have been hauled up to have hulls cleaned and painted.

The open yard is littered with beams and trestles and winches and all the odd lumber one associates with such places. This but adds to its attraction, and for a moment I imagine myself in Maxwell's yard.

A blacksmith's shop stands nearby in which iron work is being wrought for repair of fishing gear. Burly hard-faced fishermen watch the smith at work.

The fleet usually goes to sea in the late afternoon, returning in early morning for the market, so throughout the day there is fine opportunity of wandering around the wharfs, studying the various types of vessels.

I deplore my ignorance of these: but one is a large schooner-like boat with bluff bows, the strakes of the hull being painted in three tiers of colour—the top one, black; the lower, white; and the middle one either brown or green.

This partiality for multi-coloured effects extends to the sails, which often have three different colours of canvas—yellow, red, and brown—arranged in horizontal bars, the bizarre effect being yet further enhanced by numerous diversely shaped patches of other hues.

The small smacks have more slender lines, and many have white hulls. Some employ nets as well as hand gear. Cuttle-fish 131 bones lie about the deck; these indicate Italian fondness for this table "delicacy".

Beyond the shipyard buildings lies a rough green, overgrown with maritime plants that would interest a botanist, and bounded by a low sea-wall, which invites one to lean on it and gaze out idly over the Adriatic.

To the left is a long stretch of yellow sands, where surf beats in monotonously under a hot sun. A lone fisher in high top-boots is dredging the shallows for shell-fish. He comes ashore with a bag filled with Venus shells (*Venus striatula*) which he will probably sell in the fish market.

As I wander along the tide-margin I pick up such familiar molluscs as "the spoot", some small cockles, a pelican's foot *(Aporrhais pes pelicani)* and other specimens without a common by-name like *Donax anatinus*, with its glossy interior and milled edge.

But I must tear myself away from this interesting locality. I drift home for lunch via the fish market, where hopeful fishwives dangle cuttlefish invitingly before my eyes but fail to secure purchase. Other fish of unfamiliar appearance lie on the slabs, many of small size but brilliant hue, and, to northern eyes, exotic shape.

After lunch my good host takes me for a car run into the country, a farming district composed of low rounded hills, broken by intersecting valleys, one of which formed, in the war time, the seaward end of the "Gothic Line".

We are in real peasant country, where men and women work barefooted in the fields, only a few being shod with rough sandals. The people are bright-eyed, vivacious, hospitable; we visit several farms whose inmates are known to my missionary friend.

Farm kitchens are red-tiled, beam-roofed, and have raised, sometimes semi-circular, hearths, with an iron "roof" above, not unlike those seen in blacksmiths' shops in our country. Wood is the principal fuel: some kitchens also have a small charcoal oven by the side of the fire.

Furniture is mostly wooden—girnel,[4] table and dressers—bringing Orkney to mind, as did also the straw-bottomed chairs. Large earthenware flasks and flagons, however, kept the picture Italian.

The farms are approached by narrow steep winding roads that make motoring an adventure, and one has time to observe the many varieties of unfamiliar wild-flowers in the fields and on the banks by the roadside. The fields themselves defy normal modes of cultivation by horse and tractor, and long hours of work with adze-like hoes must be put in before crops can be made to thrive.

Women, young and old, do much of the work in the fields, and at night carry home huge bundles of faggots and fodder. Girls loiter by the roadside tending two or three sheep, held on short tethers. Many wear bright cotton head-shawls.

Implement sheds are often made of rough poles wattled with straw. The farm-house itself usually stands on the crown of the hill and so commands a good view of the adjacent valleys. The yard of beaten earth holds stacks of grain and straw; in one this afternoon I saw a lemon bush with ripening fruit.

May 11. Pesaro has long been famous for its Majolica ware, and today I visit a local pottery where the tradition is kept alive. I am shown round the factory—if a place where everything is done by craft of hand can be so called.

A young woman explains how river-clay is taken, put in a tank, washed and prepared for the wheel. The potter, an old master of his craft, demonstrates the making and moulding of the vessels.

The lecture continues, and I am shown how the newly-formed vessel is first coated, then first-fired, and after that outlined and painted by hand, then sprayed, and, finally, baked.

In an upstair work-room skilled girls, paint-dishes on table by their sides, bend to their delicate task of hand-painting, each specialising in a particular traditional design. They use soft long pointed brushes, made from bristles pulled out from the ear of a live ox! To a spectacled octogenarian is entrusted the reproduction of old classical designs and pictures from well-executed hand sketches.

May 12. In a small village courtyard overhung with vine I watch the homeward procession from the fields. First comes a bullock-wagon, led by the farmer, whose wife sits in the jolting vehicle. Others, family groups, follow, the women bearing heavy bundles, the man leading, hands behind back.

Sheep with swollen udders are led home by Italian shepherdesses, who, for all I know, also make the sheep's cheese that I have sampled in some farm kitchens.

May 15. An early lunch enables us to set out in good time for Urbino, birthplace of Raphael, and a small university town of some distinction, situated away up in the hills inland from Pesaro. The approach up the valley gives a striking silhouette of the city with its mediaeval walls and towers.

As we wind up the ramp-like road, look, there is another "Singers Sewing Machine" poster, of which there must be hundreds throughout the country, testifying to the passion of Italian ladies for home dressmaking.

The Ducal Palace claims the few hours we have to spare. The colonnaded courtyard is beautifully proportioned, but we must hasten into the ducal apartments with their splendid furnishings and art treasures.

Wonderful tapestries depicting scenes from the Acts of the Apostles claim immediate recognition; design and execution are marvellous. Room after room—thirty-two on the ground floor along—displays the splendour of Duke Federigo da Montefeltro, for whom the palace was built.

Richly decorated murals, doors of inlay work, wall-frescoes, exquisite miniatures, coats of arms in finely-cut stone, plaques in marble and wood, bewilder the senses with their profusion.

We step into the duke's prayer room, instinctively bending as we pass through the arched entrance—the architect saw to that; even for the duke!

Our Italian guide points out a portrait by Raphael, and also several large paintings by Raphael's father, whose work is not without interest. But I like those partly finished fresco drawings done in charcoal, which reveal masterly treatment of broad

134

tones and show how the composition of the picture altered from time to time as the work advanced. One could almost see the artist at work.

The reason for the ultra-Roman nose of the Duke—prominent in every portrait—is made plain by our guide. The Duke evidently lost an eye in battle, and being unwilling to forego his chief pleasure in life, ordered his surgeon to cut a wedge out of the bridge of his nose, so that he could squint across with his one good eye and protect his sightless flank.

Come out on to the balcony of the dome! Here we have a fine view of the rich valleys stretching out in all directions. Look, there is a 12th century fort on that nearby hilltop.

We regain the street and decide on a visit to the Cathedral. My friend speaks of the noble sculpture of the dead Christ by Cimabue, which is to be seen in the crypt. I am apathetic, having seen so many garish and sometimes repulsively realistic images in such places—but Cimabue!

The sculpture is indeed memorable: the dead Christ, with Mary standing behind, erect but with bowed head, shows a restraint of feeling that powerfully accentuates its intensity. The execution of the work is perfect: anatomists say that it is a marvel of human art. But to an ordinary observer like myself its superlative beauty and purity of form are enough.

To round off the day we go a visit into the country and I have the weird experience of walking through corn-fields by a narrow footpath and for the first time in my life beholding a pyrotechnic display of fire-flies.

I catch one, and find it to be a beetle-like insect that, if blown upon, glows with white intensity in the palm of my hand, until its incandescence reaches the size of a garden pea. In the darkening landscape they scintillate in fiery showers like miniature shooting stars. Above the edge of the hill a planet burns with steady intensity.

May 16. Tomorrow we set out by car across the Apennines.

---

[1] A hurdle of crossed slats, usually portable, which is used as a gate or fence.
[2] An occupant of Rendall's train compartment who had entertained the travellers by playing the flute.
[3] A communal ball game played on New Year's Day (and also on Christmas Day) through the streets of Kirkwall.
[4] A chest for holding meal (Scots).

ORKNEY SHELL NAMES
AND SHELL GAMES

*In **Orkney Shore** Robert Rendall recalls his early memory of sitting 'under the clay bank of a low green foreshore' on a summer's evening while his mother demonstrated shore games that she had played as a girl. One game consisted of forming farm-steadings out of stones and then using shells for animals. The names of animals in Orkney dialect were given to different shells. In this paper, delivered in 1954 before the Orkney Antiquarian and Record Society (the post-War successor to the O.A.S.), Rendall returned to his mother's game in the light of his extensive knowledge of Orkney shells and of his understanding of dialect as a manuscript of local history. He was able to show that it gave an insight into an aspect of the unrecorded social history of generations of Orcadian children.*

In addressing you on a subject apparently so trivial as our Orkney shell-names and shell games it must not be concluded that I have forgotten the respect due to our young but august Society. Written records, whether in manuscript or printed form, cover only comparatively recent history: earlier times must be deciphered from the more imperishable records of stone and metal, or from the well-nigh obliterated page of folk-speech and folk-custom. The bones and shells found in our kitchen-middens have a story to tell if only we can master their language, and local customs surviving from a distant past may help us to understand how our remote forebears looked out on life or sought to solve the problems of their day.

In Orkney, where manuscript records are so scanty, such sifting of other lines of evidence becomes essential if we are to fill in in detail the picture of past life in the islands. So I make no apology for engaging your attention with our Orkney shell-names and with those simple traditional games in which, until comparatively recent times, our native shells were commonly used.

A good number of years ago I was seeking to make a collection of our Orkney Mollusca. Not being free at that time to visit likely beaches in the North Isles, and being also desirous of stimulating an interest in marine zoology among young folk in the county, I fell upon the plan of promoting a Shell-hunting Competition among our Orkney schools. With the kind support of the late Mr James Twatt of "The Orkney

Herald" and Mr George Leonard, who donated special prizes and otherwise furthered the project, the matter went ahead, and under the aegis of the Education Authority of that day was duly carried out. Collections of shells were submitted from the various islands and Mainland districts, and though the entries were mostly of familiar species, they provided useful data regarding inter-island distribution. Perhaps the most vaulable contribution which they made to our records were local names attached to a number of species.

Here are a few: Cattiebuckie or Catabuckie, big Longneb, Crow-mussel, Horse-fish, Dog-cockle, Ku-shells, Harps, John O' Groat's Nightcap, Queen's Head, small Longneb, besides such familiar designations as Grottie-buckie, Silver Willie, Tangy-buckie, Cod-buckie, Spoot, and Kaam-shell. In an Appendix to this paper I have listed these under their appropriate scientific names, so that comparison can be made with local usage in other places. It would be highly interesting, for example, to have a complete list from our Faroese and Icelandic cousins, not to speak of one from the Scottish mainland. Sheltand will be referred to later on in this paper.

In even a cursory glance over this list one cannot help observing the number of animal names, mostly of domestic or farm animals. In the Orkney of olden times the Noah's ark of the toy-shop was unknown, but the boys and girls of those days could, without expense to themselves or their parents, stock their miniature farms (laid out with beach-stones on the links or the sand) with cows, horses, dogs, cats and other such farm stock as youthful imagination could conjure up from affinity of form between shell and animal. The analogy between the finely corrugated ribs of a cockle and a sheep's fleece was not far to seek. The blue-black plumage and broad upturned neb of the common mussel at once suggested a craa or crow. Several species appear to have sufficed for a "horse" but *Modiolus modiolus* is in my judgement the example, par excellence, of the drooping melancholy of a horse's head. The dog-whelks all have pointed nebs, though it is well to note that in the Orkney list "cattiebuckies" are also associated with well-spired shells and not exclusively with the obtuse periwinkle, *Littorina littoralis.*

The absence in the above list of such familiar farm animals as sheep, pigs and ponies made me curious to know if these also survived in local memory. Discussing this with several persons I unearthed at least a "sow" or soo-shell (not to be confounded with the Norse "sau-skjell" or sheep-shell), and a "sholtie", but failed to discover what precise species of sea-shell represented these. Probably the soo-shell was *Mya truncata*, the gaper-shell, also called the Smurslin or Smerslin, and, according to *The Orkney Norn*,[1] the Smirlin (without the internal s). The outline of the single valve strongly resembles a pig's snout. This identification is confirmed by Norse usage, to be referred to later.

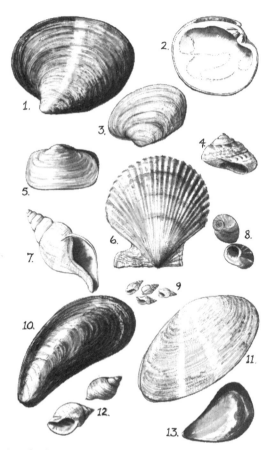

(1) *Cyprina islandica*—Koo (cow); (2) *Dosinia exoleta*—Koo (cow); (3) *Venerupis pullastra*—Koo (cow); (4) *Gibbula magus*—Sholtie (pony); (5) *Mya truncata*—Soo (sow); (6) *Chlamys* (Sps.)—gimmer (sheep); (7) *Colus gracilis*—Big Longneb (sheep-dog?); (8) *Littorina littoralis*—Cattie buckie; (9) *Nassa incrassata*—Small Longneb; (10) *Modiolus modiolus*—Horse; (11) *Lutraria lutraria*—Horse; (12) *Nucella lapillus*—Dog; (13) *Mytilus edulis*—Kraa (crow).

A lady resident in Kirkwall informed me that "Shetland sholtie" is a Deerness shell-name for the Common Top, *Calliostoma zizyphinum*. This same species, in the Competition list, was called Silver Willie or Queen's Head (South Ronaldshay). "Sholtie", without any prefix, I later found to be the Sanday form, possibly the older one, and is associated, not with the Common Top-shell, but with the Painted Top, *Gibbula magus*.

The late Councillor John Muir, who had a wide practical knowledge of our local shells, kindly gave me a list of old Orkney shell-names as being used in Sanday in his younger days. See Appendix 1 (2).

This list does not call for immediate comment, but I would refer you to *The Orkney Norn* for the study of such unusual name-forms as Smurslin, Hussif, Kraeno, and Rooklo, and leave you to your own resources for the others. Incidentally, however, it is interesting to note that Rooklo, or, as in *The Orkney Norn*, "rookler", probably derives from the Norse *rukla*, meaning a wrinkle or raised stripe. *Patella athletica* is distinguished from the common limpet by just those raised ribs or folds or wrinkles, giving it the appearance of a thing collapsed into a heap or "rookle"—to use an analogous word from the Scots.

Missing animal names invited further question. Was there a sheep-name for any Orkney shell? A lamb-shell? Had any Orcadian ever heard of a gimmer-shell?[2] Or of a shell-bullock? And if so, what shells were so named? Or were there any animal shell-names, wanting in these lists, but known to older people in the islands? It seemed likely that in the North Isles many of these old shell names would still be retained in living memory, and that further examples might be brought to light if interested individuals communicated with the local press on the subject. But no such names were forthcoming.

When the results of the Shell-hunting Competition were published, however, it so happened that our present vice-president, Dr Hugh Marwick, had come on a Norse magazine containing an article on animal shell-names as used by children in their play in the north of Norway. With his ready eye for studies of this sort and perceiving at once that some interesting parallels might be found between Norway and Orkney, he encouraged me to look further into this matter. I am indebted to him for a translation of the article referred to, which appeared in *Hjemmet* of 31-12-1925 under the title, "Farm Stock from the Ocean", and was written for children by Fishery-Consultant Oscar Sund.

This exceedingly interesting article confirmed in many instances that our Orkney animal shell names are largely derived from Norse sources, and that despite a cultural gap of centuries folk-memory has persisted when written records have disappeared. Speaking indirectly of his own young days, he writes, "The most important thing for us, however, at the beach was to collect a really good farm-stock. The dead shells took on new life when we brought them up on the grass bank above the beach, for to all land animals, tame or wild, there were quite definite kinds of shells corresponding. Knowledge of what the shells signified—that is the first knowledge children in the Nordland coast acquire, long before they know anything of a-b-c, and I believe it is the last knowledge they forget."

Then he goes on to describe the Koo-shells, but does not closely define these except as being bivalves found in the sand. Now in Orkney, as elsewhere, the koo-shells, are generally the larger white bivalves, *Dosinia exoleta*, *Phacoides borealis*, and even, if a pencilled annotation by the late Dr Iverach in a book on shells is to be believed, *Venerupis pullastra*. But *Cyprina islandica* is the species given against this name in *Cleasby and Vigfusson's Icelandic Dictionary*, as also in *The Orkney Norn*. Oscar Sund's illustration, also, appears to figure this species. To add to the confusion the late John Muir calls *Cyprina* the "horse" and *Venerupis pullastra* the Husso or Hussif, which in *The Orkney Norn* is referred to (probably more correctly) as *Mya arenaria*. This confusion is not so bad as it seems, for any white shell even faintly suggesting the body of a cow evidently sufficed to stock the byre.

But Oscar Sund goes on the describe something which so far I have been unable to discover in Orkney. He says, "Now all bivalves have two shells, and so these naturally represent male and female of the animal class they denote—the right shell being 'he', and the left 'she'. But as a farm stock should consist mostly of 'shes', it was necessary to slaughter most of the oxen, rams, and bucks. The slaughtering was performed by crushing the shells with a hammer or stone."

His horse-shell is the same species as our own, *Modiolus modiolus*, of which he says, "It is much fished (scraped) and salted for bait to be used for winter codfishing, and further south is called 'orskjell' or 'vabskjell'." In Orkney this mussel is very plentiful in the String, and their shells may be found in heaps at the Point of Carness after a westerly gale. Kirkwall fishermen used to drag the String for them just as described above.

Other confirmations are found in: the Gris, *Mya truncata;* the Kat, *Littorina;* and the Bu-hund (farm-dog) *Littorina littorea.* The common mussel, however, our Kraa-shell, was their "goat", an animal evidently not so familiar in Orkney. The common cockle was their sheep, the spiny cockle, *Cardium echinatum,* being distinguished as "the Spanish ram". The scallop was the "Hane" or cock. A "bear-shell" and "reindeer" are also mentioned, but these need not concern us in Orkney.

The "dogs" were differentiated as farm-dogs, shepherd-dogs, and hunting dogs: there were even great Bernards and Newfoundlands. Dog-fights, among the dogs themselves and also with wild animals, called sometimes for separation of the combatants, and thus provided another lively feature to the fertile imagination of youth. When looking over the Shell-competition list I had been a bit puzzled how to account for "the big longneb" and "the small longneb", as none of the other names seem to be merely descriptive of the shells themselves, but to refer to the creature of which the shell was the appropriate symbol. The small longneb, I observed, stood for *Nassa incrassata.* Then I noticed that in Herr Sund's Norwegian list the "pointed-nosed" shells stood for shepherd-dogs, or collies. Can it be that our longnebs have the same reference? "Langnefr" is a familiar Icelandic adjective. I should here like to put on record that in Birsay, not so very long ago, the small longneb was commonly pierced and strung together as a necklace of beads.

Since I began to write this paper I have at long last been able to trace an animal name which had eluded my search for years and which represents a very important beast in farming economy, namely, the sheep. Enquiries after sheep-shells, sau-shells (the Norse form), lambs, and rams, drew a complete blank, but the other day, up in Birsay, I chanced to ask some friends if they had ever heard of a gimmer-shell, and at once got the answer, "Oh yes!" The shell proved to be the smaller varieties of the scallop shell, not, be it noted, *Pecten maximus,* the Harp-shell. Now these smaller pectens are not so far removed from the cockle, and have the same ribbed corrugations suggestive of a sheep's fleece. So it would appear that while cockles represented sheep in Norway and in districts where sandy beaches prevailed, the small pecten took its place on rocky shores with sandy inlets—a habitat in which cockles are infrequent, but these plentiful.

One other rather intriguing identification was made. In the Icelandic dictionary already mentioned is a list of Shell-names, including Gymbr-skel, Ku-skel, Aethu-skel, Kraku-skel *(Mytilus edulis)*, Skel-kussi (shell-bullock), and Baru-skel, the latter having its specific name appended as *Cardia testa cordata pectinata*, a pre-Linnean form of nomenclature, now quite obsolete.

In going over some of these names in Birsay and asking if any similar ones were known there I got an immediate response to Baru-skel, but was told that it was called the barrel (pronounced *barrul)* shell. I was rather suspicious about accepting this identification so I asked what shell it was. The reply came, "Not a very common shell hereabouts, but a round one with wavy bars on it." Closer questioning, however, brought out that it was probably *Venerupis rhomboides* or *Venerupis pullastra,* but to clinch the matter I afterwards produced these shells and had my identification confirmed. Baru, in Icelandic, means "waved", but until the exact species of the Icelandic baru-shell is determined it is difficult to know why it was so named. Further local enquiry produced the pronunciation "Bara-shell". To me this seems to settle any doubt of its being the same shell-name, whatever the identification may be. It seems rather remarkable that this unusual ancient name should have survived, even in corrupted form, in living memory down into our own day.

Though not immediately connected with the subject of this paper, some shell names with ecclesiastical associations may be noted here. The Lady-shell or Lady-limpet, likewise called the Mary-shell, appears to have been a widely diffused name for the smooth limpet, *Patina pellucida.* This is that little horn-coloured semi-transparent limpet found on the fronds of *Laminaria* at low water mark. Over its apex are drawn two wonderfully clear blue lines that give peculiar grace and beauty to this small mollusc. The shell must have been so named in honour of the Virgin Mary, as also were many of the more beautiful objects in other branches of nature. In Norway are found such names as Mary's gold-shoe, Mary's Garter, and Our Lady's pincushion, the latter being the common spiked sea-urchin. The Lady-shells appears to be a name only: so far as I can find it was not used in any folk-custom. Curiously enough, the same little shell is known in Birsay as the "Bishop", and *Capulus ungaricus* as "the monk's cap". It seems rather a coincidence that in a district which once possessed a monastery, and which also was the seat of the ancient bishopric, these two shells should still be known by these particular names, "bishop" and "monk's cap". Among German shell-names is a tropical mitre-shell called *Papstkrone*, the Pope's crown or tiara.

There seems little reasonable doubt that many of these Orkney shell-names are direct survivals from our Norse period, bearing as some do the ancient verbal and phonetic form, and also in most instances standing for the same domestic animal. For some, however, a broader geographical reference must be admitted. Dog-cockles and horse-mussels are a commonplace in England, and Scotland has cattiebuckies and dog-whelks, just as we do. But even allowing for such more general usage, there remain sufficient to form a side-note on our link with the heroic age of Norse history, when throughout our islands we shared the folk-customs of the north and spoke the Northland tongue.

Animal shells must obviously have been used in some kind of children's game. Their simplest use would have been to form farm-stock in miniature steadings constructed from beach-stones on the shore, in much the same way as children to-day play at houses, or younger folk in our larger cities play at shops. Indeed the memory of such play has not entirely vanished from our islands, as older folks can confirm. This may seem to you a very unsophisticated form of play, but as evidence of racial and social propensities, it is all the more valuable on that account. The habits and temper of a people are perhaps nowhere so faithfully reflected as in the games the children play. We only have to consider our troubled and war-distracted modern world to see that! Bren-guns and pistols! That the children of our Viking forefathers should have amused themselves with model farms may appear strange to folk who have been accustomed to think of the Northmen as principally being ruthless, swashbuckling adventurers, enemies of all peaceful living. One has only to read the sagas to see how deeply farming economy entered into their normal mode of life. Armed migration of farmer settlers gives perhaps a truer picture of Viking invasions, and if these shell-names and shell-games mean anything they point in the same direction. It has been suggested to me, not altogether facetiously, 143 that their raids into southern lands were really a sort of primitive shopping expidition necessary for obtaining luxuries which the sterner conditions of their northern homes could not reasonably be expected to provide. The technique of modern export and import trade in relation to local social economy had evidently not still been mastered!

Discussing these animal names at home some years ago, my own mother happened to say that as a girl she had indulged in this sort of shore-play, and that also she had taken part in a farm-game in which chuckie-stones (or bob-stones) had served as a sort of dice in the various moves, which she described as "putting the coos in the stall", and "putting the pigs in the stye." Evidently there was a whole series of such operations, regulated by the play of the chuckie-stones. For stalls of byre and stable the fingers of the left hand were spread apart, and held point downwards, tips on the ground. Likewise, when the four fingers of the left hand were held together and, with the thumb extended apart from them to form a cave, placed on the ground, there at once you had an excellent pigstye; and we may be sure that the grice[3] were tumbled in without undue ceremony.

Further enquiries locally about this game led to some interesting information, confirming the fact of its having been played in the islands, but leaving gaps in the exact manner of play. The late William Traill of Holland was enthusiastically interested in the matter, and spoke much of having seen such games played in his younger days. Councillor John Muir took the matter up, and with his usual pertinacity did not rest until he had unravelled the whole manner of play.

Unfortunately it was never committed to paper. Once, during an idle moment, he showed me all the moves, especially the chuckie part of them, which consisted in manipulating with uncanny skill five pebbles or bob-stones from the palm or back of the right hand, seriatim or simultaneously, picking up from the ground or catching from the air, according to the prescribed modes of play, of which there were some seven or eight. But I could never get the game rightly related to the movements of the various animals, which, I understood, had to be thrust into their houses when the chuckie-stone or stones were in the air. For several reasons I am now persuaded that this particular game is quite distinct from that associated with the animal shell-names, and also that the animal counters must have been bob-stones. The game is much more widespread, and seems to have been known in places as far apart as Greece and Canada, though in the latter its introduction might well have come from northern immigrants.

By this time a number of fellow-Orcadians had become interested in elucidating some of these problems, and none more so than my friend Dr Ronald B. Mooney, who for several years has kept me posted up with all sorts of unexpected references in books and in occasional literary papers to animal shell-names and to the chuckie-game. It is to him that I am indebted for a significant reference in Egil Skallagrimsson's saga to "three silent dogs of the surf-swell", given as reward to Egil in praise of his poetic skill in verse-making. The lines are worth quoting:

> The wielder of keen-biting wound-fowl
> Gave unto Egil the talker
> Three silent dogs of the surf-swell,
> Meet for the praise in his poem.
> He, the skilled guide of the sea-horse,
> Knowing to please with a present,
> Gave as fourth gift to young Egil
> Round egg, the brook-bird's bed-bolster.

These were clearly "token-gifts", and do not necessarily mean that Egil used his three "dogs" as counters in a game, though games of skill were indulged in by the Northmen, as we shall see. In a footnote, the translator, Rev. W. C. Green, remarks, "The lexicon says it is an allusion to Icelandic children's play, who put pebbles for animals." But if the lexicon be that of Cleasby and Vigfusson, as seems almost certain, the transcript therefrom is not strictly accurate, the lexicon, under *gagarr* (dog) refers to "the ever-mute surf-dog" of Egil's Saga, and adds, "probably from a custom of Icelandic children who in play make shells represent flocks and herds, *ku-skjeljar* (cow-shell), *gymbr-skjeljar* (lamb-shells) and put one shell for a dog." So that Egil's "dog" must be considered a shell, and not a mere pebble, though these, too, were used as counters in quite another context.

Dr Mooney also gave me some other references to Norse games, which I transcribe here for those who wish to look them up.

(1) "The story about the Chess Player with a sore toe   145

and the kittens is given on p. 186 of Vigfusson & Powell's Icelandic Prose Reader. The word translated by 'chess' may mean backgammon or some other board game."

Later: "I noticed that the story of the kitten and the chess-player is given in Laing's translation of Heimskringla—in the Saga of Magnus the Blind—page 337 of the Everyman edition."

(2) *Poetic Edda in the Light of Archaeology*, by Birger Norman (1931 Viking Society).

"p.80 gives an illustration of backgammon board, men, and dice."

(3) Saga Book of the Viking Society, Vol. XI, part I, 1928-33, pp. 82-83.

"A Gaming-Board of the Viking Period found in Ireland."

"The game is on the principle of Fox and Geese."

(4) *The Story of Raud and his Sons* (Payne Memorial Series No. 2), pp. 29-30.

"In connection with a crucifix seen in a dream it is stated, 'You saw . . . the toes of one foot placed over those of the other, as when children make rams with their fingers.' This sounds a bit like one of the shell games you describe, there is a footnote on p. 32 referring to an Icelandic book containing a description of the game."

In subsequent correspondence Dr Mooney collates various references to the chuckie-game, some including allusion to domestic animals, and coming from widely scattered sources.

(1) *The Folk-lore of Chios*. P. P. Argenti and H. J. Rose (Camb. Univ. Press 1949).

Chapter XV—Children's Games. pp. 1012-1013.

The PARAPETROS

Each girl holds five small round stones in the palm of her hand which she tosses in the air and tries to catch on the back of the hand; the order of play is determined by the number of stones balanced, the one with the most starting. Four stones are then thrown on the ground, one being retained in the hand and then tossed up; while it is in the air, with the same hand they must grab the four stones that are on the ground and catch the one tossed before it reaches the ground. Then one stone is again tossed in the air and the four stones on the ground are grabbed one by one, each grab being preceded by the tossing and catching of a stone that is retained in the hand; this is repeated, grabbing two by two, then three and one and then all together. The next stage is to form a "bridge" on the ground with the thumb and index of the left hand, accompanied as previously by the tossing and catching of one stone and sliding the stones under the "bridge", first one by one, then two by two, and then three and one, and then all together. If the pebble tossed in the air is not caught, the girl loses her turn and the one who succeeds in doing the various operations with the fewest breaks wins. At this game either two have a "single" or four play as partners a "double"; partners are called *amparid.*

Footnote—This word usually means the hold of a ship, also a granary or storehouse.

This exceeding lucid description of the game, with its two sets of four variants, recalled at once in vivid fashion Councillor Muir's exposition of the game as played in Orkney, and also, in part, recollections of it given me by my own mother. This cultural bridge between Greece and Orkney is somewhat amazing. Dr Mooney wrote yet again on this course, as follows:

> A friend in Liverpool told me he had read an essay by Prof. D'Arcy Thompson (Prof. of Zoology at St Andrews) on *Greek Children's Games,* and that he thinks there was something in it about throwing up pebbles from the back of the hand and trying to catch them as they fell. I have not seen the essay, which is in a collection published as *Science and the Classics* by D'Arcy Thompson, Camb. Univ. Press 1940. I do not know whether it deals with Ancient Greece or Modern Greece.

One last reference sent by my indefatigable and informed friend tracks the game to America. He happened to be speaking in a friend's house in Edinburgh on these Orkney shell names and shell games, when all at once the daughter of the house, who had been evacuated to Texas during the war, interrupted to say that the American school children played the same kind of games, not with sea-shells, but with six-pointed metal stars which are sold 12 for 5 cents. They play all sorts of games with them, one being, strangely enough, "Putting the Pig into the Pen", where the "Pen" is the cave formed by holding the hand palm downward on the ground, fingers close together but a space between the thumb and fore-finger—the very game demonstrated to me by my mother years ago. The metal chuckie-stones were like teetotums, two of the six branches being pointed, and four having knobs at the end.

Similar games are reported from quite a number of places in this and other countries. One hesitates to say that it has come down from prehistoric times, but the wide range of its distribution makes it seem to represent at least a very ancient tradition, and not merely a local usage. After all, was there not some kind of playing dice found during excavations at the Broch of Aikerness? Who can tell how far back folk-custom may go?

But it may be noted that the "animal" moves in the chuckie game (of cows, pigs and horses) seem to be a distinct Orkney usage, and it is certainly noteworthy that the stalls of the stable or byre, formed as already described, are exactly four in number, corresponding to the four "playing-counters" of the five chuckie-stones.

I am anxious, however, to make clear that the Orkney shell-names dealt with in this paper belong to a context quite distinct from that of the chuckie-game. At first, because of the animal terms given to the four bob-stones, I was misled into thinking that in some way the games were closely associated. Now I think otherwise. The animal shell-names point to a Norse origin: the animal bob-stones are merely playing-counters as used by Orcadians in a more widespread game.

In recording these scanty survivals of folk-custom I realise how incomplete a narrative I have been able to give you and can only plead that my material has provided me only with broken sentences of an almost forgotten but tantalisingly interesting story.

APPENDIX I

(1) Shell Names from "Orkney Herald" Shell-collecting Competition:

Cattie-buckie, Catabuckie—*Nucella lapillus*, the Purple Shell (but more likely *Littorina littoralis*).

　Crow Mussel—*Mytilus edulis*, the Edible Mussel.

Horse-fish (Stronsay)—*Venerupis pullastra,* the Carpet Shell. [Personal enquiry later in Stronsay supplemented this identification. The horse-fish there is more generally *Lutraria elliptica,* but see Muir's list for Sanday under Husso.—R.R.]

Dog-cockle (Birsay)—*Venerupis pullastra,* the Carpet Shell.

Cow or coo shell—*Dosinia exoleta* and *Phacoides borealis.*

Big Longneb (Birsay)—*Colus gracilis,* the Spindle Shell.

Small Longneb (Birsay)—*Nassarius incrassatus,* the small Nassa.

Lady Limpet, Lady-shell, Mary-shell—*Patina pellucida,* the Pellucid Limpet.

Grottie, Grottie-buckie, Grotto—*Trivia monacha,* the European Cowry.

Silver Willie, Queen's Head—*Calliostoma zizyphinum,* the Common Top-shell.

Silver Willie—*Gibbula cineraria,* the Grey Top.

Whelk—*Littorina littorea,* the Periwinkle.

Tangy-buckie (Eday)—*Littorina littoralis,* the Obtuse Periwinkle.

Cod-buckie, Cattie-buckie (South Ronaldshay)—*Buccinum undatum,* the Waved Whelk.

John O' Groat's Nightcap (Birsay)—*Capulus ungaricus,* the Fool's Cap.

Spoot—*Ensis ensis,* the Razor-fish.

Harp—*Pecten maximus* and *Chlamys* (sp.), the Scallop Shells.

Camb-shell—*Sepia officinalis,* the Cuttle-fish.

(For detailed comments refer to "The Orkney Herald" of 7/11/1928).

(2) List of Shell Names supplied by Councillor John Muir.

Smurslin, Smerslin—*Mya truncata,* the truncated gaper-shell.

Husso, Hussif—*Venerupis pullastra,* the pullet rock-Venus or carpet-shell.

Yog—*Modiolus modiolus,* the horse-mussel.

Kraeno, Craa-shell—*Mytilus edulis,* the common mussel.

The Horse—*Cyprina islandica,* the Icelandic Cyprina [doubtful: more likely the otter shell *Lutraria elliptica*—R.R.]

Fan, Fantail—*Ensis ensis,* the sabre-case *solen.*

Slaevry-buckie—*Buccinum undatum,* the waved whelk.

Rooklo—*Patella athletica,* the rough limpet.

Tammy-norrie—*Capulus ungaricus,* the fool's cap.

Hornie—*Turritella communis,* the turret-shell.

Kaam-shell—*Sepia officinalis,* the common cuttle.

These names are all from the island of Sanday.

(3) List of Shell Names collected by the Writer:

Sow or "soo" Shell—Probably *Mya truncata,* the Truncated Gaper Shell.

Sholtie, or Shetland Sholtie—*Calliostoma zizyphinum,* the Common Top-shell.

Gimmer Shell—*Chlamys* (vars.), the smaller Scallop Shells.

Barrel, Bara-shell—. . .

The Bishop—*Patina pellucida,* the Pellucid Limpet.

The Monk's Cap—*Capulus ungaricus,* the Fool's Cap.

NOTE—The scientific names used in these lists and throughout the text are those found in the revised LIST OF THE BRITISH MARINE MOLLUSCA by R. Winckworth M.A., from The Journal of Conchology, Vol. 19, No. 7, and further emended in Vol. 23, 131-134, of the same Journal.

APPENDIX II

Shetland Shell Names

Some notes on Shetland Shell-names have been sent to me by Mr T. A. Robertson M.A., Lerwick, joint author with John J. Graham of the recently published GRAMMAR OF SHETLAND DIALECT AND USAGE. He remembers having played with shells in childhood, but cannot now identify the actual shells with animal names. He remarks, however, that "our kye were usually 'poags', our sheep 'cockles' or 'culyicks', our lambs limpits (sic), our horses 'crab-backs'." That cockles should have represented sheep is extremely interesting to know, as this corresponds to a like identification from Norway.

Among the other names sent, the following are of special interest.

Leddie-wylk (Lady whelk)—A species of Top-shell, *Gibbula cineraria*, our small silver-willie. This name should be considered alongside our Orkney one, Lady Limpet, *Patina pellucida*.

Smislin (Orkney—smurslin?)—Jacobsen has, as in Orkney, smirslin or smerslin, and adds in query, "The name is due to its white shell?" Neill in his "Tour through some of the islands of Orkney and Shetland" (1806) says, "The smurlin or smuthlin is the *Mya truncata.*" The omission of "r" or "s" from the middle of the word may indicate corruption in local pronunciation. James Stout Angus in his Glossary of the Shetland Dialect gives smirslen.

Yoag—*Modiolus modiolus*, as in Orkney.

Kufi—*Venerupis pullastra*, the Carpet-shell. This is the same species that Dr Iverach marked as a koo-shell, and I suspect that there has been some confusion in phonetics here. Has "kufi", as distinct from koo-shell, ever been used in Orkney? Jacobsen refers "kufi" to *Cyprina islandica*, and its derivation to the Icelandic kufr=rounded top or something roundish and raised in the middle, which exactly describes *Cyprina islandica*, our Koo-shell. The possible transference of meaning from rounded-shell to koo or cow shell is an interesting point and, incidentally, relieves me of the necessity of explaining how this species shows resemblance to a cow.

Culyick—Mr Robertson sent a specimen, which proved to be *Dosinia lupinus*. Neill remarks about this name as follows: "The culleoch (sic) is the Tellina rhomboides, and the same name seems to be sometimes applied to *Venus erycina*, and *Mactra solida.*" Neill was sound in scientific identification, being Secretary of the Natural History Society of Edinburgh, and would have observed the looseness of common identification in the case of these white bivalves, so similar in appearance.

Mr Robertson also sent notes on a Shetland game, which, while not directly concerned with the subject of this paper, seems too interesting to omit. I give it in his own words:

> I remember the late John Nicolson telling me about a game that was played with little bits of peat. One child sat

in the corner with little bits of peat arranged in a half-circle. He held in his hand a 'fettle'. The other children stood round, and one would approach and say:

I FRA ALENAS
FAAN UD A SHENAS
OULD TUN A KIDMI
GLO FIT A GIRMI—
Göd be here, and what's dis at you're döin?

He would then snatch up a piece of peat and run away. The child with the fettle would run after him. If he was touched by the fettle, he had to take the first child's place.

Mr A. T. Clunas told me that this game was played in Unst, and that there the child says:

I came fae the Hielans to da Lowlans
Seekin sheep, gazlins, and swine,
A'm lost my peerie aulie-paunie
An' I warren he's no among dine.

I wish to express my thanks to Mr Robertson for this information.

---

[1] Dr Hugh Marwick, *The Orkney Norn* (1929).
[2] *gimmer:* a year-old ewe.
[3] *grice:* a young pig.

THE SUPREME IMPORTANCE AND POWER OF THE GOOD LIFE

The relationship between God's grace and the individual's good works, between gospel and law, is a classic problem in Christian theology. The Reformers of the sixteenth century stressed the priority of grace in the Christian life. Forgiveness, not the quality of one's life, was the ground of God's acceptance of humanity. This left their theology open to the accusation that it undermined morality. Certainly the existence in Scottish literature of characters such as Burns's Holy Willie and Hogg's Robert Wringham, show that there were those, in Scotland at

152

least, who were willing to use Reformed theology as a cover for their misdeeds. The tendency to stress God's acceptance of the individual and ignore the need for personal sanctity is known in theology as antinomianism. The opposite extreme is that of legalism: the individual has to earn merit with God before being acceptable.

Robert Rendall felt that the Christian Brethren were not immune from sometimes having a cerebral faith that left the individual's life untouched. His solution to the problem was that of the Evangelical tradition to which the Brethren belong. He went back to the apostle Paul and established the necessity of forgiveness, but demonstrated that in Pauline thought Christian morality, 'the good life', was equally necessary as its consequence. Perhaps E. H. Broadbent, from whose **The Pilgrim Church** *(1931) Rendall quotes, was not entirely fair to Luther. For Rendall's understanding of the Christian life as one of liberty echoes that of Luther. Both were followers of Paul in thinking that Christianity frees men from a condemning conscience, and at the same time engages them in the free service of others and of God.*

This essay first appeared in 1951 as an introduction to a series in **The Witness** *by Rendall entitled 'The Good Life'. The expanded form which appeared in* **The Greatness and Glory of Christ** *(1956) is the one given here.*

St. Paul, pre-eminently, is the preacher of grace. He proclaimed without reserve God's free forgiveness, bestowed solely because of His favour toward us in Christ. No preliminary conditions were imposed, no pledges taken, no exceptions made that salvation was available to all without distinction. The Gospel met men simply as sinners before God, and on the ground of the sacrifice of Christ announced forgiveness of sins to all who believed on Him.

In our desire to preserve inviolate this all-important truth of 'grace', and to deny salvation by human merit, we may unwittingly abjure the word 'good' as descriptive of a certain manner of life lived by particular persons. Is it not written, we say, that 'there is none good, no, not one'?—overlooking that it is also written: 'Barnabas was a good man and full of the Holy Ghost'. True indeed, before God all are sinners, but also true that sainthood, if it means anything, involves goodness. 'A good man' means that profession of faith has wrought a change in the life and a new direction taken that has become habitual.

153

The apostolic writings lay great stress on the practical teachings of the faith, not, of course, as the ground of salvation, but as its outward evidence. Mere profession, however orthodox, avails nothing without 'fruit'.

The later writings of Paul urge with increased plainness the supreme importance of godliness in life and character. His instructions to those whose duty it was to care for the flock are explicit on this point:

'If thou put the brethren in remembrance of these things, thou shalt be a good minister of Jesus Christ, nourished up in the words of faith and of good doctrine . . . but refuse profane and old wives' fables, and exercise thyself rather unto godliness.'

'Strive not about words to no profit.'

'Shun profane and vain babblings.'

'Foolish and unlearned questions avoid, knowing that they do gender strifes.'

'Preach the Word . . . reprove, rebuke, exhort with all longsuffering and doctrine.'

The apostle seems to have acquired a strong aversion from all questions that only ministered 'strife and unruly talking', and had no practical issue in godliness of life. In 'proving' all teachings thus, he but followed the test laid down for those by the Lord Himself, 'By their fruits shall ye know them.'

'Sermons take not from men's applause renown;
The people's practice is the preacher's crown.'

The attraction which early assemblies[1] had for earnest-minded Christians came as much from the quality of the lives of those who composed them as from theological disputation: we think at once of such names as Robert Chapman of Barnstaple, George Muller of Bristol, Anthony Norris Groves, and the beloved Dr. Baedeker—men whose godly devotion and Christian character have left their mark even on our own generation. If assemblies today cease to produce those whose lives are characterized by like 'saintliness', all claims of 'sainthood' will not secure continuance of vital testimony.

In our day 'doctrine' has come to be thought of almost

exclusively as abstract truth, subscribed to intellectually, and capable of theological expression. But when dealing with this concept (truth held in mental consent) Scripture almost invariably terms it 'faith' rather than 'doctrine', and its substance 'the faith', reserving the word 'doctrine' for teaching that bears on the practical life of the believer. 'Doctrine', in other words, is the inculcation of the good life.

Things contrary to sound doctrine (I Tim. 1.10) are things that belie profession: they are not vagaries of misbelief (though they may rise from these), but are the abominable practices listed in the two previous verses. The way in which the New Testament describes the word ('sound, or healthful, doctrine'; 'the doctrine that is according to godliness'), and the contexts in which the word is found, confirm this ethical and moral connotation. Matters of faith are believed: doctrines are practised.

Nor is this emphasis on 'the good life' just Pauline truth: it is insisted upon with equal force and pungency by all the apostles—by John and by Peter; by James, the Lord's brother; and also by Jude. Their epistles are not only manuals of Christian faith but of Christian doctrine, and do not hesitate to describe in forthright language the way in which believers are to walk.

To Jewish converts such teaching was no novelty. They had been under a law which governed daily conduct on all points, and on receiving Christ as their Saviour and Lord they must instinctively have asked how they were to deport themselves in their new spiritual environment. 'What shall *we* do?' was the recurrent question asked of John the Baptist by his followers, and he answered them in plain language touching the manner of their daily lives. These were the fruit of repentance.

But to produce these fruits it is necessary first to have a personal experience of the grace of God in Christ. The good life is not the result of law-keeping, since fallen man has no power within himself so to live. Only in response to grace, only by the experience of the new birth, only by the indwelling of the Holy Spirit, can men bring forth fruit to God.

Therefore keeping in mind the fundamental fact of 'grace', let us consider what contrary views Paul had to face in proclaiming his message. First, there was that of religious formalism, taken by the pious and orthodox Jew, who was afraid that the Gospel of 'grace'—with its abandonment of the law as an instrument of righteousness—would be subversive of the very foundations of morality. Paul had a deep and sympathetic understanding of this view, having himself been an ardent Pharisee, excelling his fellow-countrymen in his zeal for the law. These devotees of 'the Jews' religion' made the good life the strict observance of a legal and religious code, and consequently became rigid formalists. Not infrequently they developed a hard censoriousness against those who were transgressors or who differed from them in faith and practice. They were among Paul's bitterest opponents. In his epistle to the Galatians—and, in lesser degree, in that to the Colossians— Paul counters their teachings.

But, secondly, there was another and less honourable type of opponent with whom Paul was obliged to contend. These, in native evil-mindedness, put a wrong construction upon the message, and while consenting to 'grace' construed it as a licence for sin. They falsely reported Paul as saying: 'Let us do evil that good may come' (Rom. 3.8), thus slandering the apostle and distorting his message. Paul's indignation breaks forth against so corrupt a perversion of the Gospel. 'What!' he exclaims, 'shall we continue in sin that grace may abound? . . . Shall we sin, because we are not under the law but under grace? God forbid!'

The epistle to the Romans is a reasoned exposition of the Gospel as 'a way of righteousness', both as justification before God and as holiness of life before men. The great end of Paul's exposition is that the saints might live worthy of the Gospel they professed, and that not only in proper church relations but in the common walk of life. The sixth chapter, in particular, is designed to counter any tendency toward Antinomianism, or slackness of life combined with Christian profession. Though incidentally a discourse on baptism—and it is generally read as such—its primary intent is to urge the obligation of the good life upon all who profess to have died unto sin and become alive unto God.

Over against both legalism and licence Paul sets that noble but all too frequently abused word—liberty. For Christian freedom, while opposed to a hard strictness that puts men in bondage, gives no permission 'to do as I please', but is a free response to the goodness of God, recognizing in right living the thing that honours Him. This life does not consist only in observance of religious ordinances, nor is it merely a strict regard for legal rules of conduct, however excellent, but it is a life grounded in faith and lived in the power of the Holy Spirit, producing fruit 'after its kind'.

Thus the good life is grounded in God, and fulfils itself in the climate of Christian liberty. It is antithetical both to religious legalism and to Antinomian licence—those twin enemies of the true faith. Also, it is not to be confounded with humanism, that modern (and ancient!) substitute for super-natural grace. Man thinks to achieve goodness in the strength of his own powers, intellectual and moral, aided, it may be, by religious fervour and ceremonial rites, and so comes to burden himself and others with obligations that oppress the mind and weigh down the conscience. Or, in revolt from this, he claims to be a law unto himself and accountable to none, and so comes to live either in proud isolation or to abandon himself to a selfish and undisciplined life of pleasure. Those, however, who have submitted themselves to the perfect law of liberty, despite many a fall through sudden temptation or unwatchfulness, neither have the hard unloveliness of legalism nor lapse into the careless arrogance of the self-willed.

Careful reading of church history confirms the necessity of re-affirming this balance between grace and godliness. In his *Pilgrim Church*, the late Mr E. H. Broadbent frequently adverts to situations in history where a false balance was made between one or the other. Writing of the extreme emphasis laid by Luther on faith apart from human works—an emphasis necessitated by the corruptions of the Roman church—he observes:

> 'Luther emphasized the teachings of the Apostle Paul more, those of the Gospels less, than the old churches of believers; he pressed the doctrine of justification by faith, without a sufficiency of the balancing truth of the following of Christ which was so prominent in their preaching.'

And, quoting Staupitz's protest to Luther, continues:

> 'Christ help us that we may come at last to live according to the Gospel which now sounds in our ears and which many have on their lips, for I see that multitudes misuse the Gospel to give liberty to the flesh. Let my entreaty affect you, for I was once the pioneer of holy evangelical teachings . . . It is the fashion now to separate

157

L

from evangelical life, as though it were possible to have real faith in Christ and yet remain unlike Him in life. Oh, the cunning of the foe! The evil spirit tells his fleshly Christians that a man is justified without works and that Paul preached this. This is false. He did indeed speak against those legal works and outward observances in which, through fear, men put their trust for salvation, and he strove against them as useless and leading to condemnation, but he never thought evil or did anything but praise those works which are the fruits of faith and love and obedience to the heavenly commandments, and he proclaimed and preached their necessity in all his epistles.'

Later reformers than Staupitz found it neccessary to curb this same tendency to be 'safe and careless'. Can we today claim that like admonition, cautioning us against easy compliance with evangelical truth without a corresponding care for evangelical living, is not a paramount need both in private consciences and in public ministry?

---

[1] The Christian Brethren have usually avoided calling their congregations 'churches' because of the word's confusion between building and people. They have preferred to call them 'assemblies'. The plural is often used as a synonym for the movement as a whole. Rendall refers here to a number of the founders: R. C. Chapman (1803-1902), renowned for his personal qualities; George Muller (1806-98), who ran several orphanages in Bristol; A. N. Groves (1795-1853), a missionary, generally acknowledged to be the first of the 'Open Brethren'; and Dr F. W. Baedeker (1823-1906), a missionary in Eastern Europe who worked among Russian prisoners.

THE FLOSS, WESTRAY c 1935

BIRSAY'S FORGOTTEN PALACE

In the Middle Ages Birsay was an important religious and political centre. It was probably there that the bishop had his earliest seat and certainly Christ Church in Birsay was regarded as the senior church in Orkney. It was there that Earl Magnus was buried after he was killed in Egilsay in 1116. It was there too, according to the **Orkneyinga Saga,** *that the reluctant Bishop William the Old tested some of Magnus's bones by fire and when they turned to gold was persuaded of the Earl's sainthood. Several months later Gunni, a farmer in Westray, was told by the Saint in a vision, "Tell Bishop William that I want to leave Birsay and go east to Kirkwall." St Magnus's bones were taken in a grand procession to Kirkwall, stones being set up to mark the resting places. The building of a new cathedral in Kirkwall had already begun* **circa** *1136/7 and the Saint's remains were interred there. The episcopal seat and the centre of power were also transferred to Kirkwall.*

The archaeological remains Robert Rendall writes of here were, he felt, those of the early Bishop's Palace and not those of the palace built in the sixteenth century by Earl Robert Stewart, the ruins of which still dominate the village. Birsay has a long history of human settlement. The various phases can be seen on the Brough of Birsay, a tidal island, and Rendall was familiar with the Brough's archaeology. The site of Christ Church is disputed and the Brough is one of the possible locations. But in this essay Rendall was advocating a mainland site, under the present Parish Church of St Magnus. He was led to this belief by strong local traditions among his Birsay friends. The remains underlying their gardens and houses had an additional interest for him as a fragment of an ancient wall formed part of Janet Couper's house, Lower Palace, where he went on holiday as a boy. She remained a life-long friend and it was to her that **Orkney Variants** *was dedicated. Although Rendall's archaeological discoveries were made in the twenties and thirties, this essay is an example of his continued interest in the subject. It first appeared in* **The Orkney Herald** *in April, 1959.*

Birsay tradition and personal examination on the spot confirm what our scanty written records have to tell us regarding the site of the now vanished Bishop's Palace at Birsay. These notes collate what little is yet known from local tradition about the site.

The Orkneyinga Saga informs us that "William was Bishop
of the Orkneys, and the Episcopal seat was at Christ's Kirk in
Birsay." When the Cathedral was built in Kirkwall the Bishop's
seat was transferred to that town.

In a holograph note, written probably about 1870, by
George Petrie, former Sheriff Clerk of Orkney, in the
possession of Dr Hugh Marwick, the following observations are
made:

> The Parish Church stands on considerable founda-
> tions, and though now bearing the name of St Magnus the
> change would be naturally accounted for by the fact that
> St Magnus was buried in Christ's Church, Birsay . . . and
> became the Patron Saint of the County. The foundations
> of a chancel at the East end, of dressed red freestone, were
> dug up only three or four years ago. Remains of the
> connection of the N. and S. walls of the Chancel yet
> project from the East wall of the present church, which
> was thus very probably the East end of the Nave of the
> original *stately* church . . . The Chancel has been 18 ft.
> wide outside. What length from E. to W. cannot now be
> ascertained . . . and here tradition says he was buried, and
> thither the Messigate or Church Road leads. [The line of
> the Messigate is still a living memory in the district.—
> R.R.]

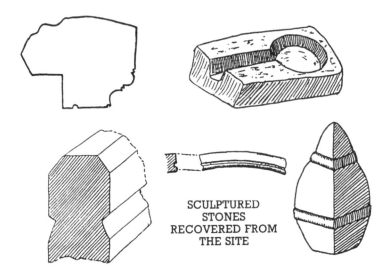

SCULPTURED
STONES
RECOVERED FROM
THE SITE

Till lately there were Remains of a considerable
building with freestone dressings, said to be the Bishop's
Palace, to the South of the Parish Church of Birsay,
between the present manse [now the Old Manse to the
south of the church—R.R.] and Parish School [now the
old schoolhouse.—R.R.].

Storer Clouston in his "A History of Orkney", page 312,
speaks of "His [the Earl's] 'New Place of the Yards' (so called
in contradistinction to the much older Bishop's Palace) . . ."
This places the site of the old Bishop's Palace in some close
proximity to that of the Earl's. In local speech the word "Place"
is still used phonetically for "Palace", though now employed to
describe the village as a whole.

Under "Sites in Birsay" the "Inventory of Ancient
Monuments in Orkney" has the following entry:— "BISHOP'S
PALACE—No structural remains are visible."

To these preliminary statements drawn from written or
printed sources I wish to add some notes from personal
observation and local tradition.

People in the immediate vicinity refer to the "Lower
Palace" in distinction from the Earl's Palace. Older people in
the district still speak of "going from the Lower Palace to the
Ummost Place." The Lower Palace was, by strong local
tradition, the *Bishop's* Palace.

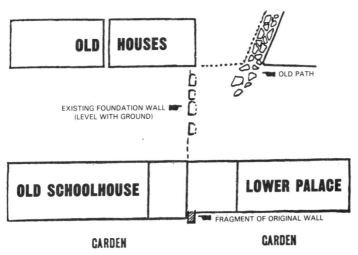

Plan of existing foundation wall.

The Palace is said to have stood on the ground to the north of the burn, near the cottage occupied by Miss Cooper, and extending (in part at least) along the site of the old schoolhouse, with their respective gardens. The garden ground, when dug, discloses a complex of old foundations with harl-pointed stones and heavy blocks, some of them being of dressed freestone. The occupant of one of them, Mrs Comloquoy, has come on many of these. Among the stones recovered is a yellow freestone finial, a cope-stone, a slop drain, and a number of fluted facings for windows or doors, also in freestone. Built into the wall of an adjacent shed is a long, narrow curved archstone, of red freestone, such as might have been used in an ambry. The original buildings must have been substantial.

The largest scale Ordnance Survey Map, second edition of 1902, bears the symbol of "an ancient site" on these two gardens, and is marked "Site of Bishop's Palace".

The cottage referred to above has from long living memory been called "Lower Palace". Behind its back wall is what remains of a thick wall pulled down some years ago during repairs to the cottage. A small portion still remains, about 3ft. high, 27ins. wide, and projecting 3ft. out from the wall of the cottage. This, because of its old associations, was deliberately kept and not demolished when the alterations were being made, the reason being that it was the last visible fragment left of the Bishop's Palace.

162   JANET COOPER'S HOUSE & TEA-ROOM, THE LOWER PLACE, BIRSAY   c.1930

On 2nd April this year Dr W. Douglas Simpson, during his visit to Orkney on University Week, found time to come up to Birsay, and among other things to inspect this site. He confirmed that the fragment of wall "had the stones in position," and he also saw some of the dressed stones. Accompanied by Mr Evan MacGillivray we went round to the front of the cottage, and in exact alignment with the side of the wall at the back of the cottage we could trace the line of the same wall right across the open square, near the very spot indicated by Petrie. It consists of heavy blocks now serving as a road surface. The fragment of wall at the back appears to be bonded in through the side wall of the cottage and is situated at a mutual gable between two buildings.

The plan of the Earl's Palace, preserved in the General Register House, Edinburgh, shows the site above referred to as "Barns and Stables", but at the date when this plan was made the old palace must have been long in ruins, and these barns and stables must have been later constructions, made possibly from material taken from it. It is interesting to note that the roughly flagged path shown in the plan still exists: it runs along the back of Robert Harvey's house and Heimdahl.

The proximity of the site to that of the old church makes a bishop's palace on it reasonable. And if we accept the evidence of a "lower" and an "ummost" (upper) palace as being both in the same vicinity, then the existence of the Bishop's Palace bears corroborative evidence for the present St Magnus Church being on the actual site of the ancient Christ Church. Incidentally, two of the so-called "Magnus Stones", one on the north side of Birsay (a high visible one destroyed during the last war) and the other in a field between Skippiegeo and the Palace, are in a straight line with the Church.

The almost entire disappearance of the walls of the old Bishop's Palace is accounted for by the strong probability that the stones from its ruins, especially the dressed ones, would have been quarried and adopted for use in the "New Place of the Yards", and the remainder used in the construction of later secular buildings. But while the later built Earl's Palace might indeed have taken dressed stone from the old site, it seems scarcely likely that such stones would have been carried from the later building and buried in the gardens of the schoolhouse and cottage site.

In the summer of 1957 a stone bearing the arms of Bishop

Stewart (circa 1511) was found by Miss Comloquoy, St Magnus Guest House, in a wall of what had been the inner righthand corner of the passage entrance into the Earl's Palace. The face with the arms lay uppermost and was covered with lime mortar. It had been built *into* the wall, the flat edge of the stone being part of the wall face. It was of red freestone. The stone was given into the custody of Mr Albert Thomson and is now in the Cathedral, where there is another, almost a facsimile, of the same arms, but having additional framing. The Birsay stone shows a mitre with ribbon over a shield bearing the coat of arms. Hossack in his "Kirkwall in the Orkneys", page 64, illustrates the Cathedral stone.

The old foundations of harl-pointed stones, the dressed freestone, the wall line of old building near the area of ground indicated by Petrie, together with the evidence of place-names, confirm the persistent local tradition that somewhere on this spot stood the ancient palace of the bishop of Orkney before the see was removed to Kirkwall. Lest these facts of tradition and of local memory should become lost to posterity I have thought it well to place them on record, and to leave their interpretation to wiser heads.

The obscure complex of foundations on this and adjacent sites, the virtual disappearance of recognizable walls, the building reconstruction over an extended period of time, make identification of the sites of ancient erections very conjectural. New facts may be brought to light that will modify, or even correct, those here presented: meantime, it seems worth while to preserve in this brief form what might otherwise soon be forgotten.

JAMES LINKLATER

James Linklater (1876-1951) had an important place in Robert Rendall's imagination. He was the subject of Rendall's poem 'Old Jeems', and, along with Willie Harvey, was one of Rendall's chosen companions in 'Doun at the P'lace'. In his youth Linklater had travelled widely, sailing on foreign voyages, but when Rendall knew him he had a small croft, and spent his time fishing,

beachcombing and acting as the local handyman. Linklater was a
member of the Kirk abune the Hill, and in him Rendall found the
simplicity and freedom that he felt was characteristic of the Orkney
crofter-fisherman. This prose description of Linklater is from
Orkney Shore (1960). The sea-fishing episode with which it
begins—showing Rendall's recurring feeling of participating in
ancient rituals—first appeared in **The Glasgow Herald.**

Fishing cuithes from the rocks is an art still practised in
Orkney. Fishing rocks are traditional stances made use of as far
back as Norse times; how much further, no one knows. Birsay
has many such rocks, especially on the North Side, a district
whence, only a generation or two ago, was drawn the crew of
many an arctic whaler.

The coast here is a line of low cliffs, below which long
black reefs of rock extend seaward, broken up by narrow 'geos'
or inlets, and intersected by tidal channels where seas swirl
treacherously or explode impetuously.

On the grassy verge of a gap in the cliffline—called Skippiegeo—are scooped out some twelve boat-nousts[1] holding several
small fishing boats, and so preserving a thousand-year-old
tradition.

Cuithe fishing—the "cuithe" is the Orkney name of the
coalfish, as likewise "sillock", "dundie", and "saithe" in other
stages of its growth—is generally done from small skiffs and
yawls. Long wands (with three feathered hooks at the end of
their stout lines) are trolled from the stern as the oarsman
slowly rows the boat. When sea fishing is impossible, tides
suitable, and the wind in a good airt[2], local fishers man the
rocks.

Seasoned fishers know each ledge and reef, and are familiar
with every combination of wind and tide. James, an old Cape-
Horner and one-time ship's carpenter, native of Birsay,
beachcomber, inveterate fisherman on sea and loch, a man who
was skilled in all jobs requiring manual dexterity and who daily
kept an eye on sea and sky, was one of these. Many a time have
I stood with him, now on that flat table of rock at Stinkaniegeo,
now on the outermost point of Longaber, and sought to fill a
cubbie.[3]

The events of one memorable day remain fresh in my
mind. In thought I still see James coming out of his house. He
quietly sets two wands against the stone eaves of his small

weather-scarred cottage, and I know that we are going to the rocks.

Nothing is said, but we shoulder our cubbies, tuck our wands under the left arm (thus leaving the right free for action), and set out past the woodpile and along the boulder track below the dyke of the old kirkyard.

Eyes on the ground, but with an occasional lift to the sky, we cross the winter fields, on to the banks of the north shore.

James halts at the cliff-edge and surveys conditions, takes a glance to see how fellow-fishers on particular stances are getting on, says nothing, but moves slowly and deliberately toward a narrow cliff track, and descends by heel-steps in the clay bank to the firmer footing of the rocks below. He has selected his spot.

At this stage he picks up a chunky stone and tosses it over his shoulder into the cubbie: I do likewise, asking no explanation.

We thread our way seaward through a wide expanse of shore. James leads, and keeps to a predetermined route—one, doubtless, taken by his father before him, and by untold generations of Birsay fishermen. It follows, roughly, an invisible contour line avoiding all sudden bad gaps, and is usually a narrow ledge with a higher supporting rock on the one side, and a flat ridge below on the other, against which we steady ourselves as we go, grasping our wands firmly in both hands and using the butt as a fulcrum.

As we traverse a broad flat ledge, slippery with weed and sea-slime, James edges his steps along particular crevices that criss-cross the uncertain surface. As I hesitatingly follow after him I have the sense of taking part in some strange esoteric ritual going back to prehistoric times.

The rocks can be dangerous, not only because of slippery shelves sliding down into deep water, but also because with a rising tide (the best one for fishing) the insidious rise of water soon isolates any outer rock, and should a heavy sea be on, incoming waves soon make a wide gap against safe crossing. James knows just how long it is safe to remain on a stance, and times it closely—for with him to be too early is just as great a waste of time as being too late.

We undo the line, free the hooks, and begin to cast; but the fish are slow in 'working'. James feels for that chunky stone and begins to knock limpets from an adjacent rock and to pound them into fragments, from time to time throwing handfuls into the sea. He might have had with him, as on other occasions, 'leepid' limpets—that is, limpets steeped in hot water to make them softer and more palatable.

He straightens himself, again grasps the fishing wand, and patiently renews his casting. Not without result—for a single sillock or two, attracted by this miraculous shower of food, follows the flies tentatively: some are caught.

But it is later in the afternoon, on toward evening, before a true rise comes, when—perhaps for half an hour or so—we take fish with each draw, frequently three at a time, the line being swung inward, the fish deftly unhooked and tossed into the cubbie, and another cast made over the lucky spot.

It is now that the art of the true seafisher comes into play, for there is skill in nicking them at the end of the draw by a last-chance twitch of the line, not too hurriedly—a sort of follow through that lifts the fish out of the water at the last moment. It takes practice, but an old hand like James works without haste, yet with an efficiency that soon half fills his cubbie with perhaps three or four score.

I resort to the baited hook, fish deeper, and am rewarded by larger though fewer fish, one a red-scaled monster with a swine-like snout, which James retrieves for me after it has become entangled in some overhanging weed.

A bit further out some sea trout are jumping. We have the thrill of hooking two of these, in deep water. Their wild plunges defeat our attempt to hold them, our wands having fixed lines: eventually the gut gives way. One big fellow takes refuge in a bunch of seaweed, and were I willing to wait until the tide falls (and so forgo the use of my rod) I might win him later, for the gut is tough; but in too violent an effort to coax him out I snap the gut. Only non-fishermen scoff at 'the big one that got away'! James tells me that his father caught a four-pound sea trout from this very rock.

We fish until darkness makes it difficult to see the white of the flies, then by unspoken consent make up our wands and retrace our steps over the rocks. Familiar reefs are now blurred and indistinct, and the value of the traditional route at once becomes apparent.

We leave our rude knocking stones behind us: they have served their purpose, and James's instinctive economy of effort will not permit him to burden himself with even a needless stone: I suddenly see why he only lifted his at the foot of the beach where the reefs began and no further loose stones would be found.

We slither up the cliff track and reach the fields. A single gleam lightens the west, and as we trudge homeward we find ourselves in harmony with each other and with the world about us.

Back at the cottage, we count our catch, gut the fish, and put them in brine. After a day or two the sillocks will be spitted, head upward, on wires, and long rows of them hung over James's open hearth, with its peat smoke swirling up the lum. Larger fish will be hung on the cottage wall on fine days, or split and exposed to the air on wooden boards out of reach of the cats; and, finally, pressed between stones. A store of fish will be laid up for future use.

Again I see glaucous cuithes arrow through the limpid water after the flies: again I experience the thrill of sharing in an agelong tradition and in the secret excitement of that passage across the rocks. Yet the track is not marked save in the minds and memories of men throughout successive generations. It cannot be wiped out by the rage of storms or the tide of winter seas. The whole activity itself is free from modern rationalisation and if it has wisdom it is that of primitive man and not of civilised convention. Perhaps this is why it is so supremely satisfying in an age when almost every action of our lives is ruled by the exigencies of some sacrosanct social purpose.

BIRSAY FARM c 1920

*   *   *   *   *   *

James's woodpile at Birsay became something of a legend. It had been gathered over the years from almost daily combing of the beach and though a strictly private possession it had a general interest for everyone who saw it, local or visitor. For he not only added to it planks and hatchcovers, driftwood and other kindling, but all sorts of flotsam and jetsam: lost gear from fishing vessels, bits of iron and scrap, wicker baskets, lumps of yellow wax, fish-boxes, bottles and fragments of rope—anything that could be made use of in his simple yet richly variegated way of life. "Jeemie's woodpile" was a forum, too, for local gossip at the end of the day, and there was always a plank laid handy so that the parliamentarians could sit down and lean against the pile while they discussed the doings of the day.

James was deliberate in all his movements, and proportioned his labours to just what was required for the work in hand. He had an uncanny knack of finding some practical use for every item in his miscellaneous *omnium gatherum.* Outside his cottage door was stacked a secondary woodpile that once had been a rude scaffolding of trestles and planks, and which now had become smothered over with odds and ends, and formed a depository for any smaller unusual objects that he might pick up in the course of his beachcombing (everything was grist to Jeemie's mill). In it, too, he kept his cuithe wands and an old much mended trout-rod that he used for fishing with in the burn; in the summer he always had in it a tin containing worms scoured in sphagnum moss, ready for taking to the loch when need be.

His cottage interior was an enchanted cave. Save to a privileged few (and I count it my good fortune to have been among them) entrance was denied. Many a time I have passed through the doorway, threaded my way to the high-backed Orkney stool at the far side of the hearth, sat down, and let my eye wander round to take everything in. On my right I looked down on the stone hearth with its carefully replenished fire of peat and small wood kindlings. It was stacked round with beachwood. The chimney walls were varnished black with soot and cast a glassy gleam into the room. Smoke curled up past rows of dried sillocks that hung suspended from long wires strung across the chimney stone and reaching up as far as a blackened mantelpiece on which stood a strange assortment of tins and canisters. Further along the wall was a dark corner festooned with oilskins and other gear, and in front of it, facing a table set against the small cottage window, was Jeemie's wooden stool where he sat when having his meals. The window was set in a deep recess caused by the thickness of the cottage

169

walls: for the cottage had a double wall, James having upon a
time decided to build for himself a new house outside the frame
of the old one, which then he was to demolish from the inside.
Thus he planned in his own ingenious fashion how to build a
new house on the same site without having first to vacate the
old one. This was never completed, so the window space was a
deep embrasure or port that, within and without, became a
handy niche for all sorts of oddments.

On my left, a tier of tool-chests and a heavy chest-of-
drawers served as a partition, screening the back part of the
room, which contained mysteries that even I, an intimate friend,
was never able to penetrate. Between these and the inner door
stood the box-bed. This had in front of it an old sea-chest, for
James had sailed far and wide in the old wind-jammers and in
his time been round the Horn. A few books always lay on the
lid of this chest, bought at some sale or other; they included
several in Greek and Latin, which made them to James though
he might not be able to read a word of them, objects to be
treated with respect and shown to intimates.

The rafters were a world in themselves, full of nooks where
all manner of things were stowed. Up there, between the beams,
James kept his cheese and other eatables likely to attract mice or
rats: there, too, he laid up his fly-rod for the loch, his landing
net, and a small round leather seat pad that he sat on in the
boat.

The table was littered with his more recent finds from the
beach, and was piled with boxes and jars. And there was James
himself, seen in profile, sitting at his table having tea, and
before him, on the middle of the table, a small hand-lamp
precariously balanced on a pyramid of boxes and throwing a
yellowish light upon the faint aura of peat reek that hung about
the room.

The shadows danced here and there as the fire flickered
from time to time, and again I would let my eye rove round the
walls or move over the stone floor to the dark corners under
the table. The whole was an establishment which, in spite of its
apparent disorder, served the daily routine of James's leisurely
but purposeful life. Beyond, through the entrance passage, was
his work-bench with his large assortment of tools: for James was
the handy man about the Place and was constantly being called
upon to do some repair or other. His woodpile contributed to
such labours, and it was a standing convention that while he

would give away a piece of wood to a neighbour without any monetary recompense, if he had touched it in any way with a tool a charge had to be made.

Loch-fishing displayed James's skill as a boatman. With effortless ease he kept the lie of the boat so as to gain every advantage of wind or ripple; and he knew the shallows of Boardhouse and Hundland to a stone. Almost weekly during the summer months a friend and myself usually had him with us as boatman in one or other of these lochs, and our baskets of fish were due in large part to his keeping the boat on a good drift or in skirting the shallows round the edge where trout were wont to lie. On two memorable days in Hundland in August 1946 we caught between us 105 trout, all on fly, the last one taken in the evening weighing 3 lbs. 1 oz.

James had infinite patience when the loch was dour, and was always anxious that we should "fish on". I well recall the last occasion when he was with us on Hundland. It was the end of the season, and the day's fishing was over. We landed on one of the small islands before making homeward. It was the last lingering hour of the day. Sitting on big lichened stones at the edge of the water we silently ate our 'pieces' and drank our thermos tea. There the three of us were, old James, Dave and myself. Casting out the dregs of tea from our flasks we rose and prospected the little islet, one of a chain-like group at the lower end of the loch. James picked up a few wing-feathers (he had a use for these), and with a boylike simplicity strange to see in an old man gathered a posy of water-mint. I did likewise and added to them single specimens of a few other wild-flowers found in late bloom. They stood all winter in an Italian majolica vase: when next spring came they had become dull and colourless, with leaves shrivelled and dry, their fragrance gone. James, too, had gone, and lay buried beneath the turf. That last day of the season remains like a faded flower, preserving in thought moments and motions that will never return.

---

[1] *noust:* landing-place.
[2] *airt:* direction.
[3] *cubbie:* a small basket, often used for bait or fish.

THE ORKNEY SHORE

This is the final chapter of **Orkney Shore** *(1960). It shows how Robert Rendall's interests in nature, literature and religion were united on the shores of Orkney.*

With the publication of *Mollusca Orcadensia* I missed a task which had become part of my life, and though other forms of marine creatures still fascinated me I slackened off from serious study and returned to the contemplative relaxed attitude I had beside the shore in early life. Thus without losing an interest in natural science I came to make it a part of a wider enrichment. Over those who haunt our island shores there often comes an indefinable sense of well-being that lifts them up on a crest of inward happiness. An Orkney writer describes it in lyrical prose.

> As I walked downhill, over grass starred with
> tormentil to a shore where black rocks were parti-coloured
> with the yellow tangle of the sea, and the sea was still
> glass-grey, I became aware of an extraordinary physical
> pleasure. It suffused my body and possessed my mind.
> Eyes and ears contributed to it, but my lungs were filled
> with it—I breathed the euphory that blows down from an
> arctic spring.

This may indeed, as Eric Linklater affirms, find outlet in bold action, but it also expresses iself in other ways—in poetry, for example. When that foreign mood falls on us familiar lines of verse often take on strange relevance. I never see a scarfie[1] sunning itself on a skerry[2] without Duncan Robertson's lines coming into my mind.

> The yellow-footed dotterel piping run,
> The cormorant spreads his black wings to the sun.

Once, too, when sailing home from Egilsay in the 'Barabel' on a fresh afternoon in late summer, I saw what Edwin Muir saw when he sang of 'the massed islands' clustering together:

> And though all ran together in his view
> He knew that unseen straits between them lay.

172 Suchlike magic moments kindle delight in the mind, and, in

some inexplicable way, become significant. Fugitive as they are they awaken sudden recognition. But of what invisible world? *That* we cannot tell. Yet we feel them to be intuitions of ultimate truth. To capture such a moment in verse is like netting a rare butterfly.

Natural beauty evokes other forms of response. An artist does something more than transfer to canvas a record of *what* he sees; *how* he sees a thing is also important and may be conveyed in the subtlest of ways. Study one of Stanley Cursiter's Orkney cliff picures and you will realize that what is there is an attempt to set down the fleeting vibrancy of our island sunlight as it transforms sullen black lumps of cliff into something like an ethereal landscape. Look again at a cliff in the sunny distance and you will see that he is right.

So I became drawn again to the imaginative in nature and to what Wordsworth describes as

> Those shadowy recollections,
> Which, be they what they may,
> Are yet the fountain light of all our day,
> Are yet a master light of all our seeing.

Already for some years the impulse to write in verse, neglected in middle life, had come back to me. While still a schoolboy, I had composed verses that were expressions of sheer delight in being alive and of sharing in the simple joys of nature. When my brother and I went along the shore we declaimed all sorts of rhymes and couplets to the waves. Cleaning out my garret the other day I came upon some of these childish verses. They read strangely now, for though spontaneous in feeling they were trite in form, and I had little reluctance in consigning them to the fire.

Landscapes familiar in childhood when seen in later life often touch secret springs of memory and in some mysterious way fill us with those 'shadowy recollections' either of unreasoning terror or of ineffable good. Is it that in childhood visual impressions are made on us unknowingly while we are occupied with the concerns of the passing moment, and that some link between these subconscious impressions and our emotional mood at the time retains its power in the mind, so that when in later life the thing seen is suddenly presented to the eye the mood of happiness or terror returns? The long familiar curve of the far horizon seen from a Birsay cliff-top, the

173

M

green links of the north banks at Westray, stitched with yellow trefoil, a solitary man hoeing turnips in a field, a black reef of rocks sticking up out of the sea, a mere patch of seapinks—nothing is too ordinary to evoke these instinctive motions of the mind.

It is a more difficult thing, however, to regain the simple happiness, uncomplicated by thought, which we knew in childhood. Yet there must be many living in our islands, plain-living people, who without giving heed to the why and how of it live lives of ordered simplicity in surroundings of natural beauty, content with their daily lot. Not all, but some. For of this I become more and more certain that there are more folks than some may think who, not consciously 'poetical' or 'artistic', nevertheless have that sensitivity and imaginative vision which make the world such a treasure-house to live in.

These, for the most part, live and work within sight of the shore. They are familiar with tides and seasons. They work out-of-doors under an open sky—plough, do fencing, feed hens, repair outhouses, walk among their fields, attend the cattle. Work is the salt of country living: without it everything becomes insipid.

The mere 'cottage in the country' is a pipe-dream. Unless we share in its activities we cannot enjoy rural life. So with the shore. Only those can know it intimately who *do* something on it, harvest tangles, catch fish, gather whelks, study nature, or even comb the beach for driftwood. Its wholesome effect on mind and body, and on the imagination, must be incidental and unforced.

The shore dweller has companionship with the free world of nature. There is always life and movement, birds flying about, waves breaking, salt winds blowing, an occasional seal in the bay, seapinks and other flowers giving colour to the foreshore.

The shore, too, holds links with the past. The knowes and kitchen middens, the churchyard by the shore which is such a feature of the Orkney landscape, the rude graves of shipwrecked sailors, the boat nousts at the head of the beach, the flagstone quarries—these all bind us with our forebears and make up a pattern of local history reaching back for generations.

I have looked on other shores and felt their charm and colour. At Pesaro in Italy I have admired the peculiar grey-green of the Adriatic and sauntered along the tide-mark picking up shell after shell. It is a shore that now has my heart. But even there I was haunted by the tumbling seas of Orkney.

It is hard to tell what gives our Orkney shores their distinctive character. It has something to do with the light. Edwin Muir noticed this and spoke about 'the Orkney landscape and the Orkney light.' In one of his poems he describes 'the still light on the sand, the shallow water clear in tranquil air.' It must have been this translucency of light into which the islands sometimes swoon that gave rise to the legend of the vanishing isles. It was also Edwin Muir—no provincial, but a man who knew cities and had travelled widely through Europe— who said in a letter sent me just after his return from Prague: 'still, Orkney is the best place. Happy are they who never leave it.'

Like him, but in a different way, I early felt the contrast between Glasgow and Orkney. His was an exile from island to city, an expulsion involving a journey back; mine, an early escape into freedom, and in the islands themselves, to its edge by the shore. Glasgow had been to me, boy as I was, a vast terror-filled jungle, which by its very immensity and swarms of people was too much to take in. One had to be alert. But when I came to Orkney, life became more manageable. I found myself moving within a recognizable pattern of living. People were spaced out, and there was a landscape that allowed distance. This was life as it should be.

Yet from Glasgow I carried away with me memory of the wider world of men and affairs. This gave depth and perspective to my sight of green fields and leisurely moving people. Innocent pleasure by shore and meadow kept at a distance, but did not abolish, that other world, which, despite its intimidating whirlpool of civic business, had compensating values in its cultural wealth. I remembered (and even took a pride in knowing) what city life was like; but I found contentment in my new surroundings. And now, in later life, I find it where I found it as a boy, and realize my good fortune in having lived my life in Orkney.

Country living need not be uncultured. It leaves room for literary and scientific interests, and if we become too absorbed in these, nature will recall us to herself. An evening will come, and suddenly there is the moment of vision. Afterwards, we say to ourselves:

But I have seen, like treasure long concealed,
A sudden radiance break from evening skies,
And everything on sea and shore and field
In flawless essence move, without disguise;

And watched with awe, beside the old sea wall,
In the hushed stillness of a summer night,
O'er land and sea an innocent beauty fall—
The setting sun had touched the world with light.

What is it that so moves us as we stand on the shore and look out over the ocean? Not thought alone, or even imagination, but natural response to an immensity and wealth of life exceeding our power to grasp. "The sea! The sea!" The exultant shout of Xenophon's soldiers when they caught sight of the Euxine after their long and arduous inland march finds an echo in the breast of everyone born within sight of the sea. Its continual motion, its potential of storm and tempest, its remoteness and mystery, its primeval birth, all combine to cast an awe upon our spirits and to soothe the inborn restlessness of our hearts. There is healing in the sea for mind and body. "The sea," said Euripides, "washes all ills away."

It provides a metaphor for our deepest intuitions. "Though inland far we be, our souls have sight of that immortal sea, which brought us hither." The simple pleasure which a field of daisies at Pipersquoy gave a boy of seven was multiplied a thousandfold when he came upon the inexhaustible treasures of the Orkney shore.

In the sea and its inhabitants the Psalmist found an image of the ever-present providence of God. "So is this great and wide sea, wherein are things creeping innumerable, both small

MARWICK BAY

and great beasts. These all wait on Thee." And again, in words that gather up all that need be said on so marvellous a work of Divine creation, "The sea is His, and He made it."

[1] *scarfie:* cormorant or shag.
[2] *skerry:* an isolated rock in the sea.

THE ORKNEY ANTIQUARIAN SOCIETY

The Orkney Antiquarian Society was formed in 1922 with the Venerable Archdeacon Craven as its President and Hugh Marwick as its Secretary. It became important as a focus for the intellectual activity of the islands and for preserving and keeping in Orkney many of the archaeological finds that were being made at the time. The activities of the Society were suspended in 1939 but they were not resumed after the War. The artefacts that were held in the Society's Museum are now in Tankerness House, Kirkwall. Robert Rendall's short history of the Society first appeared in **The Orcadian** *in 1967. These extracts from the history describe the Society's meetings and the personalities associated with it.*

Like the seasonal changes in the playing of children's games, the cultural pursuits of an adult community are unpredictable and full of change. But unlike educational programmes, amateur interests follow no fixed rule; they have a spontaneity that adds colour and sparkle to life. Looking back over the years we can trace a pattern of local life that varied in its cultural interests from time to time. Just as art seems now to have taken a hold upon Orkney's imagination—we never seem to have had so many highly skilled artists and keen amateurs—so in the inter-war years archaeology was the dominant interest.

It was the period when Scarabrae was being excavated under the superintendence of Professor V. Gordon Childe; when the broch of Gurness and that other across the Sound were first opened; when the unique stalled cairn and other sites in Rousay were scientifically explored; when, almost weekly, in the pages of "The Orcadian", was reported a fresh find in some district or other—an underground chamber, a burial cist, some relic from a   177 kitchen midden, or perhaps a steatite urn unearthed by the plough.

The focus of all this antiquarian interest was the Orkney Antiquarian Society. This society kept a watching brief over new discoveries, published in its "Proceedings" an account of much that was being done, and co-operated with authorities in the South in a way that commanded their complete confidence. One important result of official confidence was that the Society was allowed to keep in its museum in the Library building many local finds which would otherwise have gone to Edinburgh.

A pattern of specialised scholarship emerged; each contributing member made some particular branch of local research his own, but all maintained a common devotion to the general purpose of the Society.

J. Storer Clouston explored the Norse period of Orkney history, and wrote some fascinating and highly original papers on the masonry of old Orkney houses. John Mooney became our authority on St Magnus Cathedral, and on old Orkney families. Hugh Marwick (later to become D.Litt.) not only contributed uniquely valuable papers on place-names but compiled a series of Record Miscellanies preserving scraps of local knowledge which otherwise would have been lost to memory.

These three formed a sort of unofficial triumvirate that gave scholarly standing to our Society, but they were ably seconded by others who also made certain provinces of local research their own. Their names are still household words in Orkney: John Spence of Overabist, Birsay, recorded the fast vanishing features of "Moorland Orcadia"; James Begg, S.S.C., Procurator Fiscal, wrote on "The Early Orkney Justiciary"; Provost James Flett contributed a series of papers on "Kirkwall Incorporated Trades"; Duncan J. Robertson gathered together fragments of "Orkney Folklore"; John Fraser listed the antiquities of various parishes.

We had corresponding members in various parishes. These formed a happy link between ourselves and the farming community, and kept us in touch with fresh finds in the country. As these were reported to us, members habitually paid such field sites a visit of inspection. Country members on occasion attended our meetings, among whom may be mentioned that knowledgeable personality, Peter Leith of

Stenness, and Mr Oddie of Tankerness, the latter having a special interest in flints, of which he had formed a good collection.

There was an unofficial, almost parliamentary, protocol in the conduct of the Society's meetings. Minutes were duly read, and, as a rule, approved: the chair was respected. No smoking was indulged in during the formal proceedings. There was a sort of inner cabinet composed of acknowledged 'experts', but also a sturdy row of 'back-benchers' who noted every move and were ready, when it was fitting to do so, to intervene during 'question-time' with observations that sometimes were a tacit criticism of some point raised in the paper read during the evening—a sort of watching brief, keen enough in itself, but modestly exercised. At times the persistence of a skilful 'heckler'—such as the Procurator Fiscal, James Begg—provided a stir of interest, and even amusement, but the general atmosphere of the gatherings was one of a happy band of brothers.

This discipline resulted in the maintenance of a high standard in the published papers. Even so respected a contributor as J. Storer Clouston did not escape this friendly inquisition. In the discussion that invariably followed the reading of a paper there was always a keen debate on dubious points, and many a contribution which had been submitted to this keen cross-questioning, when appearing in print in the following week's issue of "The Orcadian," showed discreet modification of points of view.

Our meetings, too, had social grace, reminiscent of Edwardian days. Members brought their wives with them, and once the formal part of the evening's proceedings was over, there was a general mingling of members, front-benchers and back-benchers mixing freely and gathering in small animated knots—a sort of 'lobby' in which opinions on the high points of the evening were interchanged. This was when the back-benchers came into their own and a happy spirit of camaraderie promoted—a mutual deference that yet was not without strongly held individual opinions. It was a 'live' Society.

After the death of the Ven. Dr. Craven, the chair of the Orkney Antiquarian Society was filled by Joseph Storer Clouston. His conduct of the meetings, no less than the precise scholarly bearing of the Secretary, gave them somewhat of that parliamentary character already referred to.

Mr Clouston was a patient listener, and while retaining a

firm grip of things, could always show humorous indulgence during a discussion. His papers were perhaps the most boldly speculative of those read before the Society, but his legal training had given him a wide grasp of competing possibilities in matters which were of doubtful interpretation. There was often keen but friendly criticism of the views he put forward. But he faced 'question-time' with an inscrutable countenance. We all looked forward to a 'President's evening'.

A Society is very much what its Secretary makes it. The O.A.S. was extremely fortunate in having one of Dr. Marwick's calibre. During his term of office he not only organised the general work of the Society, and scrutinized with editorial strictness the proofs of the "Proceedings", but with his colleagues maintained a close working relationship with fellow scholars in Scotland and Scandinavia.

The part played by John Mooney in our meetings is difficult to write about with restraint, so outstanding were his gifts and his intellectual vigour. His own highly original contributions to local historical research made a splendid addition to our "Proceedings" and later found extension in his own published works. His wide knowledge of all aspects of Orkney life—particularly his painstaking research into the history and standing of the City and Royal Burgh of Kirkwall and its ancient Cathedral—was always available to those seeking help and information. His home became a rendezvous for distinguished visitors to our islands.

During debates, though not afraid to state his views with modest frankness—he could be forthright, if necessary—he was often, until called upon, a quiet appreciative listener; and when he rose it was always to express critical pleasure in the paper

EARL'S PALACE, BIRSAY c. 1920

that had just been read. It was through his tactful encouragement that I became a member. Would I draw a ground-plan for
him of the choir of the Cathedral to illustrate a paper that he
was preparing? It was only later that I realised what must have
been in his mind all along. The possibility of finds in 'kitchen
middens' was one of the things that he was always seeking to
impress upon the minds of young people.

William Traill of Holland was the friendly gadfly of the
Society. None of us escaped an occasional sting. He came in
from Papey (as he invariably called his native isle) to see if we
were all doing our part in antiquarian research in Orkney and in
our own Society in particular. We enjoyed his banter and
occasional outbursts immensely: he was held in strong regard
amongst us. His special interest was in the building up of the
Museum, but he also loved to visit recent excavations. Once he
took me with him to make scale plans of the earth-house just
discovered at Rennibister. He initiated me into the methods
used in making ground and sectional plans in inclosed quarters:
he was, of course, a trained surveyor. His private excavation at
the Knap o' Howar in Papey gave him an outlet for his
enthusiasm. In this work he had the able assistance of William
Kirkness, F.S.A.Scot.

William Spence, a retired chemist, had a unique position in
our Society. He had a keen critical mind, a rich caustic humour,
and a somewhat sardonic mode of speech at times. He wore a
brown tweed Norfolk jacket, which somehow seemed to
symbolise the man. During the forenoon he could usually be
found in his brother's boat-building shed in St. Olaf's Lane, or
at the Library scrutinizing and deciphering old manuscripts—at
which task he was adept. While always ready to give help if this
were asked for, he avoided office, but later became our Curator.
He loved to walk out the Berstane road in the late starry hours
of winter, when he would regale his few chosen companions
with reminiscences of his experiences of London life.

Another of our active back-benchers was John Windwick,
who for a time was Curator of our growing Museum, and who
occasionally gave a short paper. As a skilled operator in the
machine room of "The Orcadian," he made a splendid link
between the editing of the monthly papers by Dr. Marwick
and their due presentation in the printed "Proceedings". He was
thorough in his work, and a favourite mode of expression when
a matter had been done to his entire satisfaction was

"Complete!"—accompanied by a circular motion of his right hand in the air.

No one who has spent a working evening with Dr. Marwick in his own home, by a fireside in winter, will ever forget the friendliness and intellectual refreshment experienced on such occasions. The Doctor dearly loved a bold devil's advocate as a sort of check for his own views on some debatable detail in interpretation. The tussle usually ended in a spontaneous mutual burst of laughter, as much as to say, Hold, that will do! I was privileged to read most of his recent works in manuscript. It was against a background like this that the whole relationship between members was given its distinctive character— there was high seriousness when it was appropriate, but also an equality in common interest that gave personal relations a delightful freedom.

This brings to mind a lighter note sometimes struck in our public gatherings—a note reminiscent of Dickens's "Bill Stumps, his mark". One afternoon I had occasion to call upon Dr. Marwick at the Kirkwall Grammar School when he was Rector there. Before I left his small office he handed me a curious stone, shaped like a human foot, and asked me what I thought it might be. But as a frequentor of our Orkney shores I did not fall into the trap. His face relaxed into a friendly grin, and he brusquely said: "I picked it up from a load of shingle on the playground. Hand it to our Curator." The evening of our next meeting came round, and, as custom was, when the formal proceedings were over, any new additions to the Museum were handed round for personal inspection. The stone was solemnly produced: member after member handled it reverently and speculated what it might be. Dr. Marwick fixed his eye upon me from the platform with a dead-pan look, as much as to say, Dare you give me away! I returned his gaze with a deliberate uncomprehending look. Of course, we confessed afterwards, and stories were exchanged of such happenings not being unknown in Edinburgh itself to the the confusion of the pundits. So we were human after all.

SELECTED POETRY
OF
ROBERT RENDALL

From
COUNTRY SONNETS
(1946)

HESTIGEO, BIRSAY

Siberian Spring

Suggested by a passage in Dostoievsky's 'House of the Dead'

Compassionate Spring has set God's creatures free
Who long have been in Winter's gloomy prison;
And out of dungeons dark how joyously
The gentle flowers of the wood have risen.

April is come! And, lo, before her tabor
As if by magic force each fetter breaks:
The mounting skylark makes the sun her neighbour,
And every living thing its freedom takes.

Throughout the land, in valleys without number,
The forest trees in fresh green leaf are found;
And shy small woodland beasts from winter slumber
Creep forth to dance and sport upon the ground.

But shackled here 'mid shameful things and rotten
God's noblest work, sin-laden, lies forgotten.

The Fisherman

Adapted from Andrew Lang's Translation of Leonidas of Tarentum

Aald Jeems o' Quoys, wha erst wi' leid and line
   Keen as a whitemaa, reaped the Rousay Soond,
And in his weathered yawl a twalmonth syne
   Set lapster-creels the Westness craigs aroond,
Nae stroke o' fortune cloured wi' bluidy claa,
   Nor glow'ring daith wi' sudden tempest mocked,
But in his wee thatched croft he wore awa'
   E'en as a cruisie flickers oot unslockt.
Nae kinsman raised, nor wife, nor weeping w'ain,
   But we, his yamils, this memorial stane.

erst: *formerly*	craigs: *sea-cliffs*	unslockt: *unquenched*
whitemaa: *gull*	cloured: *struck*	w'ain: *child*
syne: *since*	cruisie: *fish-oil lamp*	yamils: *contemporaries*

Orkney Crofter

Scant are the few green acres that I till,
   But arched above them spreads the boundless sky,
Ripening their crops; and round them lie
   Long miles of moorland hill.

Beyond the cliff-top glimmers in the sun
The far horizon's bright infinity;
   And I can gaze across the sea
     When my day's work is done.

The solitudes of land and sea assuage
My quenchless thirst for freedom unconfined;
   With independent heart and mind
     Hold I my heritage.

The Knowe

Wrecked on the ocean wave were we
  Who late were cast upon the shore,
Whence to this knowe beside the sea
  Sea-faring men our bodies bore.
But here though lodged among the dead,
  We oft, when evening falls, can feel
The laden fisher homeward tread
  With basket filled from line and creel.

Kirkyard by the Shore

In this old kirkyard lay my coffined bones,
That I, perchance, like those within these graves,
On winter nights may hear the waves
Thundering among the stones.

From
ORKNEY VARIANTS
(1951)

THE FLOSS, WESTRAY c.1900

Cragsman's Widow

"He was aye vaigan b' the shore,
    An' climman amang the craigs,
Swappan the mallimaks,
    Or taakan whitemaa aiggs.

"It's six year bye come Lammas,
    Sin' he gaed afore the face,
An' nane but an aald dune wife
    Was left tae work the place.

"Yet the sun shines doun on a' thing,
    The links are bonnie and green,
An' the sea keeps ebban an' flowan
    As though it had never been."

vaigan: *wandering*	mallimaks: *fulmars*	links: *undulating ground*
craigs: *sea-cliffs*	whitemaa: *gull*	*near the sea*
swappan: *catching in a net*	gaed afore the face: *fell from the cliff*	

By wi' the Sea

Owre fail'd tae rive in face o' angry seas
Or sit apae a thaft and lift an oar,
A'm dune wi' sea-wark. I maun bide ashore,
Bitin' me thoom, while ithers catch the breeze.
But though me joints are aald and growan stiff,
I'll bigg apae the green a steethe o' stanes,
And whummle than on tap me tarry skiff
Tae sair for shelter tae a dizzen hens.
Baith man and boat, mebbe, in spite o' weather
For twa'rthree winters yet'll haad together.

fail'd: *worn out*	thaft: *rowing-bench*	whummle: *overturn*
rive: *struggle*	bigg: *build*	sair: *serve*
apae: *upon*	steethe: *foundation*	twa'rthree: *a few*

Salt i' the Bluid

A'm bydan heem, 'at geed for lang
    Ruggan afore the mast,
Yet times me thowts they taak a spang
    Aff tae the wild Nor'wast.

On winter nights I whiles can feel
    Me cottage gaan adrift,
An' wance again I grip the wheel
    Tae the sea-swaal's aisy lift.

Whan lood swaps gouster at the door,
    An' the nort' wind tirls the sneck,
Full canvas on, we drive afore,
    As whaalbacks sweep the deck.

Spier no for siklike ferlies proof!
    Things chance when nights are lang:
The very timmers o' the roof
    Creak as we dunt alang.

bydan: *staying*	swaps: *gusts*	sneck: *latch*
'at geed: *that went*	gouster: *storm*	speir: *ask*
ruggan: *toiling*	tirls: *rattles*	siklike: *such*
spang: *leap*	whaalbacks: *long smooth*	ferlies: *marvels*
Nor'wast: *Davis Straits and*	waves (lit. *whale-backs*)	dunt: *bump*
North-West Canada		

The Planticru

Whaur green abune the banks the links stretch oot
    On tae the sandy noust, lies midway there
An aald-time planticru, smothered aboot
    In weeds—but fu' weel delled, and dressed wi' ware.
Biggid o' sea-worn boolders fae the beach
    A dyke runs roond it, lichened doun the sides,
Scarce keepan leaf and root beyond the reach
    O' winter gales and fierce Atlantic tides.

'Oors lang, an age-bent wife wi' aspect mild
    Stands gazan oot tae sea; or digs a speel,
Slowly, as if by vagrant thowts beguiled,
    And sets her twa'rthree tatties i' the dreel;
Nor kens hoo firm she haads b' siklike toil
    Man's aald inheritance o' sea and soil.

planticru: *small vegetable plot*
abune: *above*
links: *undulating ground near the sea*
noust: *landing-place*

delled: *delved*
ware: *seaweed*
biggid: *built*

speel: *spell*
twa'rthree: *few*
siklike: *such*

Shore Tullye

An experiment in Scaldic metre

Crofters few but crafty,
Krugglan doun b' moonlight,
Hidan near the headland,
Hint great congles waited.
Swiftly rude sea-raiders
Stranded, evil-handed:
Scythe blades soon were bleedan,
Skulls crackt in the tullye.

Stretched the battle beachward;
Bravely back we drave them.
Een fleep fleean hinmost
Fand we maakan landward:
Him apae the hillside
Hewed we doun in feud fight—
Never kam sea-rovers
Seekan back tae Rackwick.

tullye: *skirmish*
krugglan: *crouching*
hint: *behind*

congles: *large boulders*
een: *one*

fleep: *useless fellow,*
sluggard
apae: *upon*

I' the Kirk Laft

Here i' the sooth laft's neuks sae dim,
Twa aald-time relics—Haad thee wits!
A hangman's ladder twa could clim',
A widden pulpit, geen tae bits.

Whaur ither should they than in kirk
O' guid and evil mind us a'.
Time plays, hooever, mony a quirk:
Prelate and tief are baith awa.

Haad thee wits!: *listen!*

Envy

After Lucilius

Young Magnus wi' the muckle teeth
    For very madrum's deid:
His brither sheep-thief dirls beneath
    A higher gallows-heid.

muckle: *big*   madrum: *frantic rage*   dirls: *spins*

Haad Aff, Haad Aff the Pleugh

After Heraclitus

Haad aff, haad aff the pleugh, nor saa thee seed
Here b' the knowe, whaur sleep the ancient deid,
    Aald banes hae po'er o' ill, and fegs, it's true,
That if thoo disna heed
      The Pights 'll maak thee grue.
    Haad aff, haad aff the pleugh!

haad aff: *keep off*	fegs: *faith*	grue: *shudder*
saa: *sow*	Pights: *Picts*	

The Happy Isle

After Detlev von Liliencron

The ulie-lamp reeks in the muify byre,
Whaur, ooran wi' content, twa nowt lie spraalan:
Rooster and hens claa tight apae the hallan,
Scrattan in gloondie dreams amang the mire.
The crofter's laddie wi' his shepherd's reed
Aald-farrant tunes plays tae his peerie brither,
And bairns and kye and birds aa' thirled together
Let this world's tide gang swirlan ower their heid.

ulie-lamp: *oil-lamp*	hallan: *inner dividing wall*	aald-farrant: *old-fashioned*
muify: *close, warm*	*(between living-room & byre*	peerie: *little*
ooran: *lowing softly*	scrattan: *scratching*	kye: *cows*
nowt: *cows*	gloondie: *greedy*	thirled: *bound*
apae: *upon*		

Contentment

After Leonidas of Tarentum

Look! This is Liza's but and ben,
Wi' screen o' bourtrees tae the door,
Her stack o' peats, her flag-roofed byre,
Her planticru abune the shore;
Yet 'mang her hens and hoosehold gear
She's bruck'd aboot for eighty year.

but and ben: *two-roomed cottage*   abune: *above*   bruck'd aboot: *pottered*
bourtrees: *elder trees*   gear: *goods*   *about*
planticru: *vegetable plot*

Doun at the P'lace

After Antiphilus of Byzantium

If aa' were as I would, and fate were kind,
    I'd hae the gift
O' vaigan roond wi' Jeems along the tide-mark
    gathering drift,
I would on summer mornings, aff Skaehua, haal
    the creels,
Or fish for lythe; whiles taak the oars a bit, in
    easy speels:
And, evening come, I'd maak oot by the Brough
    in Willie's boat,
As I sae aft hae deun, lang syne, content tae
    be afloat:
Or as the streen, wi' some aald fisher stand,
    and fae a rock
Catch a few cuithes—for I hae aye been blyde
    o' ord'nar' folk.

vaigan: *wandering*   lythe: *pollack*   cuithes: *coalfish*
speels: *spells*   the streen: *yesterday evening*   blyde: *fond*
syne: *since*

The Twa

After Hugo von Hofmannstal

Wi' danglan shanks and tousled hair
And whistlan owre a country tune
Intae the yard he rode the mare,
Cried, "Whoa," and louped fu' lightly doun.

She cam' oot fae the byre door
Wi' milk pails sweeman tae the brim,
And stepp'd alang sae douce and prim
A single drap ne'er lippid owre.

Yet when the lad in ilka hand
The weel-filled buckets fain wad tak,
Ere ane the tither's fingers fand
(Sae potent was their saft desire)
The twa at aince began tae shak;
And guid white milk ran doun the syre.

louped: *leaped*   lippid: *brimmed*   syre: *gutter*
douce: *sedate*   ilka: *each*

Celestial Kinsmen

After Marcus Argentarius

The winter lift is glintan doun
Wi' tullimentan stars besprent,
As were the very heavens abune
Clean gyte wi' frosty merriment,
Their lowan e'en are taakan tent
O' chiels like Mansie o' the Bu'
Whase days upon the land are spent
Ruggan wi' Taurus and the Pleugh.

lift: *sky*   abune: *above*   tent: *notice*
tullimentan: *glittering*   gyte: *daft*   chiels: *fellows*
besprent: *sprinkled*   lowan: *gleaming*   ruggan: *striving*

Plain Fare: Guid Lear

After Lucian

Hibernicus aye scowlds the lass wha bakes
Sweet savouries, merangues, and pasty cakes,
And scunnert, flytes, "Bold huzzy, wouldst
    thou dare
Tae meddle wi' a Scotsman's honest fare?"
Yet when o' oatmeal brose he's cleaned the plate
Tae glaip some venison he's naething blate,
And woodcock pie goes weel, it's finely kent,
Wi' frugal meals and soond Scot's argument.

lear: *learning*   brose: *meal and hot water mixed*   glaip: *gulp*
scunnert: *disgusted*   flytes: *scolds*   blate: *bashful*

Hinmost Days

After Richard von Schaukal

The aald man still keeps wand'ran
    Tae the brecks besooth the yaird:
He's naething noo tae lippen,
    He's by wi' it aa', he's fear'd.

Wi' fing'rs cruikit and bluidless
    He grips the heids o' corn:
He kens it's weel nigh deun wi'
    Yet bides as he wis born.

brecks: *shallow barren ground*   lippen: *expect*
besooth: *to the south of*   bides: *remains*

Winter Threshing

As within a dream,
Dim shapes flicker and fall
On the gable wall:
Spectral shadows flung
By the lantern hung
'Neath the loft's low beam.

From the mill's great mouth
Comes, with deepening wails,
Gust on windy gust,
Like autumnal gales
Whirling high the dust
After summer's drouth.

Now the golden grain
Falls like April rain:
Chaff, like floating mist
By the sunshine kisst,
Brings again the dawn
Of May-mornings gone.

Idly drifting by
To the roof's dim span,
Straw-clouds come and go:
In the barn below,
Ghostlike, moves a man,
Raking down the sky.

'Mid the winter storms,
Viewless, voiceless forms,
Bound by Nature's chain
To the circling year,
Dance in solemn train
Round Earth's mystic sphere.

In procession slow
Grave immortals go.
Move the seasons four,
As in days of yore,
With Pandean song,
Hand in hand, along.

Still upon the wall
Dim shapes flicker and fall:
Swift light-footed fauns,
Seen again in trance
In their ritual dance
On Hellenic lawns.

drouth: *drought*

The Horse-Mill

Beside the heavenly meadows daisied with stars
The planets yoked in team—Uranus, Mars,
Jove, Neptune, Venus, Mercury, Saturn, Earth—
Not saddled now to run with tightened girth,
But to the mill's unwieldy lever bound,
Wheel their enormous burden round and round.
Linked to the trees, harnessed with hame and trace,
They stumble round the tracks of cosmic space,
With slow hard step, necks bent, and flanks a-sweat
Turning yon beam, the sun for axle set.
To grind what corn in what celestial mill
Move these great Titans, shouldering onward still?

hame: *draught-horse collar*

From
SHORE POEMS
(1957)

In the Ebb

Even upon the margin of the deep
    Life spills her myriad forms before our gaze
    In tiny treasures—bright anemones,
Worms, star-fish, crabs, and little fish that leap
Across the pools. Look how storm waves heap
    A fringe of shell along these sandy bays,
    And how on golden bladderweed that sways
With rhythmic motion periwinkles creep.

I step from stone to stone, and as I peer
    Far into depths of pools inhabited
By swarming ocean creatures, I can hear
    Echoes around me of the Voice that said,
Go, have dominion over great and small,
And name all living things that swim or crawl.

Angle of Vision

But, John, have you seen the world, said he,
Trains and tramcars and sixty-seaters,
Cities in lands across the sea—
Giotto's tower and the dome of St Peter's?

No, but I've seen the arc of the earth,
From the Birsay shore, like the edge of a planet,
And the lifeboat plunge through the Pentland Firth
To a cosmic tide with the men that man it.

The Happy Fisherman

Within his little kingdom
Beside the Birsay shore
He's tilled his few green acres
For thirty years or more,
Yet even at his farm-work
He listens to the roar
Of great Atlantic breakers,
And wanders back and fore
With eye upon the weather
Until the gods restore
The longed-for hours of sea work,
Handling creel and oar.
He's ready every evening,
Cuithe wands at the door,
Returning nigh on midnight
With ten to twenty score,
And lythe, perhaps, from Marwick
To salt and lay in store.
Thus Willie, for a lifetime
Skilled in country lore,
Has ruled his little kingdom
Beside the Birsay shore.

cuithe: *coalfish*   lythe: *pollack*

The Stone Wave

On this great beach a wild
        Atlantic storm
Sculptures in stone its huge
        and wavelike form.

New Cemetery, Birsay

Struck by Death's storm, this
      churchyard's even ground
Breaks its green calm with many
      a wavelike mound.

The Miller

By day he laboured in the mill
And in the evening fished for trout:
He was a man of patient skill
Who loved his task, indoors or out;
And nothing better to his taste
Than when his evening board was graced
With new bere bannocks and a fry
Of sweet half-pounders caught on fly.

bere: *old Orkney variety of barley*

On Sigurd—

WHO GAVE A FIELD AS A GRAVEYARD

Here, in his own home field, among
      his guests,
Crofters and fishermen, old Sigurd
      rests.

Old Jeems

I knew a Birsay man, an old beachcomber
Who gathered driftwood, holding it in scorn
To lose one piece. His thoughts, like those of Homer,
Compassed the ocean. Oft by memory borne
On long sea voyages around the Horn,
He saw the storm waves sweep the high four-master,
Or caught some glimpse of shipwreck and disaster
Beyond the latitudes of Capricorn.

And so beside his woodpile he would stand
When evening came, and lost in distant dreams
Gaze seaward, motionless, with pipe in hand.
Beside him, too, now finished with their labours
Would come for idle talk his friendly neighbours:
For everyone about the P'lace knew Jeems.

Orkney

To my Uncle William

This is the land whereon our fathers wrought
   Year after year, feeling scant need to clutch
   For distant gains, since, with little or much,
They tilled their scattered fields as they'd been taught,
Or tried the sea to find what might be caught
   Of fish or crab. This was their land, and such
   Their joy therein, seeing the sunlight touch
Its evening hills, no other land they sought.

This kingdom, too, is ours, and in our blood
   Its passionate tideways run: its moorlands fill
With peace our casual eyes; and the wild flood
    Of winter haunts our ears with spells that bind
   Sea, sky, and earth in one. Each cliff and hill
    Lies like a shadow on the brooding mind.

Train Journey

Journeying homeward, from my corner seat
   I watch the view beside the railway lines.
   It passes like a film: olives and vines
Lacing the landscape; strips of sugar beet
Hoed by Italian peasants; fields of wheat
   Scarlet with poppies; strange commercial signs
   And white-washed farms. Far off, the Apennines
Shimmer, blue-distanced in the summer heat.

Beyond it all I see an island shore
   Far in the north—the land that I love best.
     Again I gather sea-shells on the Brough,
Or dream an angler's dream and drift once more
     Within my little boat, when on the loch
    Trout rise, and the wind blows from the west.

The Title

"Let Christ the King of Israel descend now from the cross, that we may see and believe."

MARK 15.32

Forth from Zion's citadel
Who is this led out to die,
As those voices rise and swell
"Crucify Him—crucify!"?
Mocking rulers make reply,
"Christ the King of Israel!"

Simon, whom they did compel
After Him to bear His cross,
Saw His anguish and could tell
How the soldiers dice did toss,
How He died to bear our loss—
Christ the King of Israel.

Hushed be every heart and tongue!
There, to save our souls from hell,
He in agony is hung,
Numbered thus with thieves among.
'Twas for us—O mark it well—
Christ the King of Israel.

Like a wounded wild gazelle,
Stricken sore and mortally,
From His parchèd lips there fell
Groans of dire extremity:
"Why hast Thou forsaken Me—
Christ the King of Israel?"

Finished what the Scripture saith
And the prophets' words foretell:
Silenced now each infidel.
See! He bows His head in death,
And He yields His parting breath—
Christ, the King of Israel.

Here, beside His cross, is found
Mercy without parallel.
This indeed is holy ground,
Let our sandals be unbound
While we linger near its spell—
Christ the King of Israel.

Praises be for what befell
On that dark and dreadful day.
Everywhere let people say
"This our guilty fears can quell:
Christ has borne our sins away—
Christ the King of Israel."

Hail we Him, Emmanuel,
Throned upon the royal tree,
Who in distant islands dwell;
And from henceforth none but He
Shall our God and Saviour be—
Christ, the King of Israel.

Thine Evermore

"Thine are we, David, and on thy side, thou son of Jesse."
                                                    I CHR. 12.18

Lord, we are Thine, the captives of Thy bow:
Fast as we fled Thine arrows laid us low.
We found Thee Friend who feared Thee once as Foe.

Lord, we are Thine, necks bowed beneath Thy yoke,
Since first Thy goad our swift rebellion broke,
And Thou Thy gentle word of conquest spoke.

Lord, we are Thine, and shoulder Thy commands
Burdens laid there by Thee, who loosed our bands
And bore *our* heavy burden in Thy hands.

Captain of our salvation, staunch and tried,
Thine are we evermore, O Crucified!
Thine are we evermore, and on Thy side.

Without God

From the German of Jochen Klopper

Without God I am a raindrop in the fire,
Without God a fish upon the strand,
Without God a sparrow whose wings tire,
And a blade of grass within the sand.
But when God calls me by my name,
I am air, water, earth, and flame.

Renewal

Look how my autumn leaves from green to gold
　　Burn in their frosty fire. Tissue and vein
　　Shiver and curl to ash: no flowers remain
On withered stem, or from the patient mould
Draw breath and on life's tree their fans unfold.
　　Twice has my summer pride waxed high; now wane
　　The gentle influences of the rain,
The sun, the earth: and death comes, dank and cold.

But fast inscalloped in the undying root,
　　Constant beyond all change of sky or soil,
Lies fenced the mystery of the living shoot—
　　Green involutions of the mind. No toil
　　Attends their weaving. Ah, would they uncoil
Again from that inmost core, leaf, stem, flower, fruit.

From
THE HIDDEN LAND
(1966)

OLD WESTRAY CROFT

Autumn Sunset

If it be so, that what I see and hear
On this autumnal coast is nothing more
Than sounding seas and rugged reef-bound shore,
Caught in the colour of the changing year—
Whence, then, transcending eye and listening ear,
Do thoughts arise within me that restore
Forgotten moods, and rouse me to explore
The hidden source of things that do appear?

Uptilted now, the sun's vast crucible
Pours out upon the waves its molten gold,
And evening light with gentle radiance falls
In benediction on the cliff's high walls;
Illuminate like these, I feel the spell
Of thrones invisible in all that I behold.

Bees on Dandelions

A few late autumn dandelions
(Golden suns in a green sky)
Lift their heads in proud defiance
Though summer's noon is all gone by.

Bees, in thin sunshine, toil and slave,
Lest hidden nectar spoils be lost
And winter lock the Aladdin cave
With secret spell and key of frost.

The Masque

The black heraldic headland lifts its shield,
  But whose device it bears no man can tell,
Though blazoned clearly on an azure field—
  And simple fishers know its ledges well.

With hollow voice the ocean speaks its part,
  Now high, now low, and once again I ask
Whose tongue it is strikes terror in my heart,
  Or lulls my grief behind that painted mask.

Why hides itself in camouflage of green
  The ancient earth, whose continents we know?
What lies invisible, and is not seen,
  In rocks and iron, water, ice, and snow?

Tiptoe in cosmic dance the mantled moon
  And her attendant stars traverse the night.
To celebrate what deed, or for what boon
  They hold these revels, none can say aright.

Vainly in tragic posture weeps the rain:
  Too like a pageant are those gestures bold.
In vain the waves advance, the winds in vain
  Flourish their trumpets, clouds their flags
    unfold.

But I have seen, like treasure long concealed,
  A sudden radiance break from evening skies,
And everything on sea and shore and field
  In flawless essence move, without disguise;

And watched with awe, beside the old sea wall,
  In the hushed silence of a summer night,
O'er land and sea an innocent beauty fall—
  The setting sun had touched the world with light.

The Floss, Westray

Within its narrow bound,
This cottage by the shore,
With dark low lintelled door,
And all the little yards
Won from the sandy shards,
Is my ancestral ground.

Its walls are crystal clear
Though built of stone and clay,
And through them still appear
(Yet how, O who can say?)
The weaver at his loom
In a bare-walled room.

Sounds of grief and mirth
Echo from what has gone.
Beside the smouldering hearth,
Sits with ravelled hair,
In her straw-back chair,
A woman all alone.

Snug in shuttered beds
Children huddle in dream:
Of things long gone they seem
The stationary proof.
Upon their sleeping heads
Rain drips from the roof.

Forefathers, distant and near,
Beyond what I can trace
Crowd around me here,
Many a forgotten face
Which yet I never knew,
Although the vision be true.

Eastern Window

Experiments in Haiku

EVENING

On a fencing post
  a grey owl sits:
    a summer day's ghost.

SUNSET

In the West, a rose
  opens—and on the waves
    petal on petal throws.

IN VIKING CATHEDRAL

Darkly on stained glass
  rooks throw shadows: long-boats
    with raven banners pass.

LAST OBSEQUIES

Hands on gunwale—to the noust
  haul this weathered yawl:
    there leave her, safely housed.

noust: *landing-place*

UNCOLLECTED POEMS
(1965-7)

The Impartial Sun

After a translation from the Persian

On meädow-girse and fields o' bere
The reip'nan sun shines doun alike—
And nourishes wi' equal care
The floo'ers apae this aald hill-dyke.

girse: *grass*   bere: *barley*   apae: *upon*

On a London Street, 1932

Faded flowers in fist,
A chain of slum children—
From summer fields long missed.

Not now can squalor stain
The pure bright image
Of that fair green domain.

In mute defiance
Young eyes have glimpsed
God's glory in dandelions,

His miracle of leaf and blade,
Bud and blossom,
All that He has made.

A Select Bibliography
of Robert Rendall's Writings

Abbreviations

EQ   *Evangelical Quarterly*
J.Conch   *Journal of Conchology*
POAS   *Proceedings of the Orkney Antiquarian Society*

ARCHAEOLOGY

'Notes on a Collection of Flints from Wideford Hill' (1930), in *POAS*, Vol. IX (1931), pp.21-4.

'Further Notes on an Orkney Flintfield' (1933), in *POAS*, Vol. XII (1934), pp.19-25.

'Notes on an Underground Chamber at South Keigar, Deerness' (1933), in *POAS*, Vol. XII (1934), pp.26-8.

'The South Ettit Flint Industry' (1937), in *POAS*, Vol. XIV (1937), pp.45-56.

'Birsay's Forgotten Palace', in *The Orkney Herald*, 21 April, 1959.

CONCHOLOGY

For a complete bibliography of Robert Rendall's conchological publications see, Nora F. McMillan, 'Robert Rendall, 1898-1967', in *J.Conch*, **26**:273-274 (1968).

'Notes on *Eledone cirrosa*', in *J.Conch*, **19**:161-162 (1931).

'*Simnia patula* (Pennant) in Orkney', in *J.Conch*, **20**:283-285 (1936).

'Traill's list of Orkney Mollusca, with special reference to *Pinna fragilis*', in *J.Conch*, **23**:327-330 (1953).

'A Survey of some Orkney Beaches', in *J. Conch*, **23**:390-394 (1954).

Mollusca Orcadensia, Proceedings of the Royal Society of Edinburgh (B) **66**:131-201 (1956).

'*Eubranchus tricolor tricolor* Forbes in Orkney', in *J. Conch*, **24**:178-9 (1957).

'A Collection of Shells from Pesaro, Italy', in *J. Conch*, **25**:241-242 (1964).

ORKNEY HISTORY

'Orkney Shell Names and Shell Games', in *Orkney Miscellany*, II (1954), pp.47-58.

'Orkney's Tradition in Natural Science', in *Orkney Shore* (Kirkwall, 1960) pp. 153-175.

Orkney Antiquarian Society: Two Decades of Local Scholarship (Reprinted from *The Orcadian*, 1967).

POETRY

Country Sonnets (Kirkwall, 1946).
'A Book of Scottish Sonnets', edited with an introduction (Unpublished MS, 1949).

Orkney Variants (Kirkwall, 1951).

Shore Poems (Kirkwall, 1957).

The Hidden Land (Kirkwall, 1966).

THEOLOGY

History, Prophecy and God (Exeter, 1954).

'The Method of the Writer to the Hebrews in Using Old Testament Quotation', in *EQ*, Vol.27 (1955), pp.214-220.

The Greatness and Glory of Christ (London, 1956).

J. B. Watson, *Our Matchless Lord* edited by Robert Rendall (London, 1958).

'Quotation in Scripture as an Index of Wider Reference', in *EQ*, Vol.36 (1964), pp.214-221.

TRAVEL, BIOGRAPHY AND AUTOBIOGRAPHY

Extracts from a Travel Diary, 1950 (Kirkwall, 1950).

J. B. Watson: A Memoir and Selected Writings (London, 1957).

Extracts from a Travel Diary, 1957-58 (Kirkwall, 1959).

Orkney Shore (Kirkwall, 1960).

ARTICLES ON ROBERT RENDALL

'Death of Robert Rendall Poet and Scholar', in *The Orcadian*, 15 June 1967, pp.1 and 3, contributions by Sheriff D. B. Keith, Ernest Marwick and John Oddie.

George Mackay Brown, 'Robert Rendall: A Modern Orkney Poet', in *New Shetlander*, No.11 (1948), pp.18-9.
'Robert Rendall', in *An Orkney Tapestry* (London, 1969), pp.163-171.

Robert Kemp, 'The Wide World of Robert Rendall', in *The Scots Magazine*, (August, 1967), pp.440-2.